LIVING A ROYAL REALITY

Discovering Your Identity, Purpose, and Worth in Christ

BY:

CRYSTAL DAYE

Copyright ©2016 by Crystal Daye. All rights reserved.

Living a Royal Reality. Printed in the United States of America.

No portion of this book may be reproduced, stored in a retrieval system, or transmitted in any form or by any means except for brief quotations in printed reviews without the prior written permission of Crystal Daye

Unless otherwise indicated, all scripture quotations are taken from the Holy Bible, American Standard Version and King James (American Version).

TABLE OF CONTENTS

Dedication 7

Acknowledgements... 10

Introduction 13

Chapter 1: Brand New Free.. 19
    My Testimony... 20
    High School Days 22
    I'm a "Big Girl" Now 25
    Turning a New Page 27
    True Conversion.. 30
    Brand New Me 31
    Brand New Free 32

Chapter 2: Accepting Your Identity 37

Chapter 3: Letting Go of The Past............................... 43

Chapter 4: Being Apart of the Royal Family 53

Chapter 5: Discovering Your Purpose 61

Chapter 6: Broken for His Glory.................................. 74

Chapter 7: Beauty in the Eyes of the Creator 79
    What Beauty Isn't 82
    What Beauty Is 82

Chapter 8: God ~~Self~~ –Confidence................................ 86

Chapter 9: Overcoming Inadequacy 92

Chapter 10: Develop a Zero Tolerance for Excuses 99

Chapter 11: Choose Your Friends Wisely.................... 103

Chapter 12: Pursuit of Purity 107
　　Why Pursue Purity? 113

Chapter 13: Act Like a Lady, Think Like Jesus 118

Chapter 14: It's Not About Us 125

Chapter 15: It's a Faith Walk 130

Chapter 16: Choose to Live Your God-Given Dream 138

Chapter 17: Living for Eternity 145

Chapter 18: For Such a Time as This 150

Dedication

This book is dedicated to my baby girl, Christelle. As I wrote this book in obedience to God, I felt motivated to be transparent because my hope is that you don't make some of the unfortunate mistakes I did.

For years, my identity and worth were determined by what society said about me. I thought education, career, being in a relationship, friendships and getting people's affirmation determined 'who I am'. It was not until I truly encountered Christ and made the decision to serve Him that I realized all I need and all that I am is found entirely in Him.

My prayer is that from an early age, you will serve God wholeheartedly. I don't care if you ever get a degree or become rich, but my heart's desire is that you will be obedient to God, fulfill your purpose and show the love of Christ to everyone that you meet.

My baby girl, you are truly a gem! I'm so grateful that God chose me to be your mother because you continue to motivate me to be a godly role model.

To all the ladies who read this book, it is my prayer and greatest desire that your life will never be the same. I pray that you will come into the full knowledge of who you are in Christ and you will truly embrace the royalty God has called you to be.

I sincerely love each of you. There is so much that God wants to pour into you and I trust that your heart will be open to hear His voice, be obedient to His commands and experience His love in a whole new way.

Copyright ©2016 by Crystal Daye. All rights reserved.

Living a Royal Reality. Printed in the United States of America.

No portion of this book may be reproduced, stored in a retrieval system, or transmitted in any form or by any means except for brief quotations in printed reviews without the prior written permission of Crystal Daye

Unless otherwise indicated, all scripture quotations are taken from the Holy Bible, American Standard Version and King James (American Version).

_____

Thank you Abba Daddy, I know I could not have done anything to deserve your favor, blessings, love, grace or mercy. Thank You My King, My Redeemer and My Deliverer for giving me a second chance. Thank You for the gifts, talents, dreams, passions and purpose you've given me to serve you in this life. I love you so much and I'm forever yours. Thank you for writing this book, I was simply a vessel but by your Spirit, I'm thankful for the lives that will be impacted.

Thanks to my beautiful, supportive and super awesome family. My parents and siblings have been truly a tower of strength all of my life. I love you guys so much and I appreciate you from the depths of my heart. I'm so thankful God placed me in this family.

Thanks to my amazing friends who truly supported me on this journey called life. I'm so thankful for all your prayers, phone calls and just the overwhelming love I've received from y'all. I truly pray for you daily and words cant express how grateful I am. I prefer not to call any names but know that I love you all very much.

To Heather Gaye, thank you for your inspiration. You were the person that helped me coin the theme 'Living A Royal Reality', for the first She's Royal Empowerment Conference in 2015. The Lord also used you to inspire me to write a book to empower women. Thank you for your obedience to encourage me to live out the call of God on my life.

To my She's Royal ladies, you guys have truly motivated me to be a better Christian, minister, sister and role model. I am so grateful for your continuous love and support throughout this journey.

Thanks to my Kingdom Family at the Berean Church of God, Kencot Christian Fellowship, Portmore Church of Christ, Pure in Heart International Ministries and Divine Exchange Ministries. Thank you for believing in me, giving me a platform to share my testimony and for all the encouragement you've given me.

Last but not least, Thank you very much to my social media family, my prayer partners, my mentors, customers, well-wishers and for all the people who continue to impact my life in one way or another. I love you guys so much!

In 2009, I got baptized, but I truly wasn't living an authentic Christian life of total surrender to Jesus Christ. Instead, I lived a lukewarm and defeated lifestyle where I was engaging in premarital sex, partying every weekend, yet, still attending church. Part of me wanted to stop living my life of sin but the world was enticing, and I thought it was impossible to give up my familiar lifestyle.

Until 2012, I found myself in a horrible place of discontentment, brokenness, and self-hatred. I did not like the woman I had become. I did not want to be the girl who looked "beautiful" on the outside but whose lifestyle was not a good example to her daughter. I was tired of feeling like a hypocrite, quoting scriptures but not looking anything like the Savior I professed I served.

So, I began to pray like never before. I sought God and cried out to Him to help me to be a better person—even if not for myself, for my daughter, my niece, my little sisters and for the many young ladies who I knew looked up to me. It was during that time of surrender, I started to discover my purpose and calling and came into the knowledge of who I was in Christ. God showed me that I was not born to live a mediocre, fearful, defeated, and hopeless life. Instead, He had a great plan for my life *(Jeremiah 29:11)* and He has given me everything I need to live a victorious and godly life *(2 Peter*

1:3). I had a new encounter with Jesus Christ and like Paul on the road to Damascus, I experienced a rebirth and my life was transformed forever. That's when I started *Living a Royal Reality*.

The fact is, when we accept Jesus Christ as our Lord and Savior, we are reborn into a royal family *(Galatians 3:26)*. Unfortunately, many of us refuse to accept this new identity, and we spend our lives being battered by the realities of life and never accepting our true potential to become the best that God has called us to be.

If you can relate to any of these "realities" such as insecurity issues, poverty, sickness, purposelessness, anxiety, frustration, anger, feelings of inadequacy, loneliness, suicidal thoughts, worthlessness, lack of self-worth, lack of self-confidence, abandonment, rejection, lack of love, betrayal, promiscuity, depression, fear, brokenness, strongholds, jealousy or heartbreak—know that you are not alone. Many of these were my realities that led me to make many poor choices and mistakes in my life, which could have led to death, but God's mercy kept me. The fact that you are reading this book means God has a good plan and great calling on your life. God wants you to know that you can live a royal reality if you allow Him to take full control of your life.

Living a Royal Reality is not a fantasy story about us living a perfect life—free of trials and tests. In fact, the reality is, this life can really rock us and take us to a place of discontentment, frustration, and even depression. Many will admit—life is a test. Daily, we are tested by unplanned changes, delayed promises, impossible problems, unanswered prayers, undeserved criticisms and unexpected tragedies.

You may often see other women and start to yearn for what they have. You want "their" relationship with God—to pray like them, to dream like them or to appear successful like them. What you haven't embraced is that you have the same access to God as everybody else through the Holy Spirit.

This is not about using the power of positive thinking to live a *"good"* life. It's not your good thoughts that will turn your life around. It is only God's power that will turn your life around. I know because I've experienced His transformational power in my own life, where I'm set apart and not conformed to the world's standard but to God's standard.

This kingdom living happens when God transforms us from the inside out. It is reflected in how we speak, how we dress, and how confident we are. The King is asking us to believe He is who He says He is, believe we are who He says we are, and then live like we believe those things! We need to stop walking in defeat! Accept that you are royalty!

The purpose of this book is not to give you some secret formula that will ensure you pass all of life's tests or convince you that all your problems will disappear overnight. Instead, I'm sharing my experiences, testimonies, and revelations of God's forgiveness, grace, and redemptive power to truly empower women who lack confidence or struggle with low self-esteem to confront their insecurities, weaknesses, and limitations. It is my prayer that you will be encouraged to live a purpose-driven life and be equipped with tools and resources to maximize your potential and to live God's promise of a "royal" life.

In *Living A Royal Reality,* we have accepted that our identity is found in Jesus Christ, and we are no longer victims or slaves to sin. We have chosen to let go of our past, fulfill our purpose, walk by faith, and pursue our God-given dreams while preparing ourselves for eternity.

We are confident that God is always with us, and He has truly equipped us to overcome all of life's tests because of His son Jesus Christ. We know that no matter how many times we've failed, He has given us the authority to live as conquerors, victors and true "royalties": we have access to all the kingdom treasures and promises.

My prayer is that as you read this book, you will start seeing yourself as God sees you. Life may take each of us on different paths, you may face different tests but ultimately, you have a choice to either live a defeated life or walk into the victory already won for you.

Chapter 1:

BrandNew Free

Royal Affirmation:
"I am FREE and not condemned in Christ Jesus."
(Romans 8:1-2)

Growing up in this lost world, you are made to believe that as long as you do what you want and live as you please, you will enjoy freedom. Independence, material success, and fame are synonymous with living free. But now, as a woman of God, I have gotten the revelation that life without Christ is a life of bondage and slavery to sin. Now, I stand on the other side and can say Jesus Christ has set me free.

> *"Who the Son sets free shall be free indeed."*
> - John 8:36

My Testimony

I was born and raised in the inner city of Kingston,

Jamaica, running the streets of Maxfield Avenue, Kencot and Arnett Gardens. God has always had His hands on my life. I escaped the stereotype and stigma of being an "inner city/ghetto girl" with multiple baby fathers, multiple children, and bleached skin. Instead, with the best upbringing my parents could provide, my siblings and I found a way out of that life by acquiring an education. However, being "educated" did not save me from living a sinful and detestable life in which I was headed straight to hell.

Being the eldest child, I knew from a young age that I needed to set a standard of excellence that my siblings could follow. I needed to be the one to provide my family with a better standard of living, so I worked hard to excel academically. From pageants, to cheerleading, dancing, and community development projects, there was nothing I didn't think I could do. We grew up poor and my parents tried their best but with four children it just never seemed to get easier. I remember attending school without textbooks, wearing one uniform for the year, wearing shoes even when the bottoms were falling off and going to school without lunch money. We didn't go on school trips or have any vacations. But knowing that our parents really tried to keep us from looking the worst allowed us to walk with pride. Thankfully, our parents raised us with dignity.

My siblings and I were not raised with a Christian background, but we knew church was a good place so we visited occasionally. We also knew that we should pray because there was a God who would protect, provide, and help us succeed. I learned about prayer at a young age. I bargained a lot with God because I believed that was how one should communicate with Him. Unfortunately, I treated God like a personal genie.

Being the eldest child and wanting to seem perfect caused me to live a double life. The "good" daughter I appeared to be at home was not the same Crystal around her friends. Around my friends, I had to deal with the peer pressure of trying to fit in, so I had boyfriends, tried smoking (that was lame), cursing, and lied a lot. This pressure started from as young as 12 years old. I was just trying to keep friends happy enough to like me. So, by high school, it got worse, especially attending an all-girls school.

High School Days

I loved my high school days (most times). I enjoyed attending the annual barbecues at school (dressing up and partying); I excelled in school (graduated with six distinctions in my CXC examinations) and I met lovely friends and teachers who I can say played a great role in helping me become the young lady I am today. On the flip side, the constant battle of trying to fit in was overwhelming. I wasn't Miss Popularity, but I wasn't a nerd and being average wasn't always bad. Except, being average and getting top grades meant that many times, I got separated from my clique, so occasionally I compromised getting my best grades so my friends wouldn't feel so bad. I wasn't really a "follower" but I wasn't quite the leader either; many times I was an outcast from even my own clique because I was not willing to engage in certain activities. By 9th grade, most of my friends started to have sex—I wasn't ready.

I had boyfriends and kissed, but I feared disappointing my parents so I managed to stick it out until after 11th grade. I started to date my first real boyfriend and everyone was having sex, plus I had completed my CXC exams so, why not? My only precaution was to ensure that I didn't get pregnant because I had too many dreams. I dreamt of becoming a pilot, chef, lawyer, and politician. I was a "*dreamer*". I really wanted to be involved in politics because I have a sincere love for people and that was the only avenue that I thought I could use to truly help people to live a better life.

By the time I got to the age of fourteen, I began partying. My mother wasn't very strict, plus, I did very well in school.

She trusted me and allowed me to go out unlike most of my friends so I became a real party animal. I didn't drink, but I would dance up a storm, I loved skimpy clothing and even wanted to enter the international dancehall queen competition. Of course, I didn't bother because I was always concerned about my corporate image, and I wanted to become the next female Prime Minister so I figured that would not be good for my reputation.

In 6th form (12th grade), my biggest nightmare happened. I got pregnant. I was faced with the decision of becoming a teen mother, giving up on my many dreams of becoming a successful woman, disappointing my parents and possibly living in poverty-stricken conditions for the rest of my life. I knew many persons at that time who had abortions, so I was able to get a referral to a doctor because there was no way I would have a child. So, at sixteen (16) years old I got an abortion.

That was hands down the most horrible experience of my life. I did not know God, but I remember praying non-stop that He would help me because the pain I experienced during the process was excruciating. So many of us women have these gruesome experiences—rape, sexual and physical abuse, having an abortion or losing a child. We believe we must keep them to ourselves because of the shame and self-disappointment that we battle with. My heart is totally broken for all the women who feel they have to be under the bondage of secrets, instead of standing in truth so we can be free and so it can free others. When I came into a relationship with Jesus Christ, confessed and repented of all my sins, I walked into my Brand New Free. According to Revelation 12:11, "We conquered Satan by the blood of the Lamb and by the word of our testimony." Far too long, we have been keeping secrets with the enemy, and he holds it over us; we walk in shame when that is not what God wants us to do. Romans 8:1 says: "There is no condemnation for those who are in Christ Jesus." I choose to believe this and so should you.

I'm a "Big Girl" Now

You would think that after my mistake, I would learn and abstain from sex. Nope! To me, it just meant I couldn't trust men and I only had me. So, I ended it with my first boyfriend. I decided not to settle down but just "play" the game and dated as many men as I wanted to. I got a job at the bank, attended a university part-time, partied up a storm every weekend, lived the "hype" girl life— I was the inner city girl "headed to the top." I changed jobs, began my climb up the corporate ladder while getting a higher education and dating any guy I wanted. I was okay—or so I thought. Until I met "Mr. Love of my life." He was nice looking, drove a nice car and he had a girlfriend (even better as I only dated guys who were in relationships so I didn't have to commit). I got very popular in my community by living a lie. The girl people saw dressed up in heels and looking all pretty on the outside, was a flirty girl who was promiscuous, clubbing, and partying five days a week. My worth and my confidence were tied up in my relationships, career, education, and appearance so even though on the outside I looked "good," on the inside, I felt so empty. So much drama followed that lifestyle. Girls kept calling me to leave their boyfriends alone, having 2 or 3 boyfriends at once, having unprotected sex, not even thinking about any possible diseases I could have caught—I had no true worth; in my head I was free to do Me!

Then in 2008, the unthinkable happened. My first boyfriend (the one who took my virginity) and who eventually became my best friend was shot and killed. I was devastated, and it truly pierced my heart. I could not understand why or how that could happen to him because he was young and full of dreams. The night of his death, we were supposed to go partying, but I felt tired and fell asleep. At 4 a.m. someone knocked on my door and told me he was dead. This really affected me, and for the first time, I felt the need to find God.

This feeling was short-lived because even though I felt empty, I couldn't picture myself being a Christian, not having sex, not partying, and giving up friends seemed impossible to do. I started visiting churches more often but had no real desire to get saved anytime soon.

Then I met a *"Mr. Nice Guy,"* for the first time, I felt like I wanted to settle down. He was ambitious, handsome, and he did not have a girlfriend! Unfortunately, I was still in a complicated relationship with "Mr. Love of my life" (the one who had a girlfriend) and it was so hard to let him go. So I did what I did best—I cheated. I dated both guys at the same time. Eventually, the nice guy found out and for the first time, I felt dirty and embarrassed. I was going around trying to let men fill a void that was reserved only for God.

Turning a New Page

By December 2009, I got baptized. This was after both guys broke up with me. "Mr. Nice Guy" found out that I was cheating on him and "Mr. Love of My Life" was now expecting to become a father with his girlfriend. My heart was totally shattered. So I ran to God because I believed only He could have healed my broken heart. I accepted that I was living a terrible life, and I was ashamed of the girl I had become.

At that time I was simply remorseful *(regretful because of the consequences but no change of heart)* about my lifestyle. I hadn't realized that I never truly did repent *(turn away from my sin and surrender my heart, mind and action to God).*

So after 4 months, I went back to the old life—lying, gossiping, partying and fornicating. I improved a bit because I just had one boyfriend (yes, I went back to "Mr. Love of My Life"). I didn't stop going to church though. I actually went to prayer meetings and bible studies but I was still clubbing on Saturday nights. You better believe, I was at church Sunday morning. However, I had a certain fear of God and refused to get involved in church activities or take communion. I knew I was living a double life, and it was not pleasing to God. I made a lot of excuses as to why I could not improve my lifestyle because I was comparing my Christian walk to other people. I saw them living the same sinful life as I was even though they were involved in ministries in the church. I also believed that I had a free ticket to heaven because I believed the motto "once-saved-always-saved." So, as long as I asked the Lord to forgive me if I died, In my mind, I would still go to heaven. I was totally deceived.

In the year 2011, I got pregnant again. It wasn't a shock

because of my lifestyle at the time. However, I figured since I was climbing the corporate ladder and most of the women I knew had one child and no husband, I could make it; my lifestyle would work out well for me. Another part of me thought about having an abortion. I was afraid of what people would say because my child's father ("Mr. Love of My Life") was still involved with his other baby's mother. Plus, the girls in my community looked up to me, and I was worried that my parents would be disappointed. This thought was short-lived because I felt I was a big woman, 24 years old with my bachelor's degree and a decent job. I also remembered attending a youth retreat earlier that year and one of the lessons that resonated with me was to never try to cover one sin with another. So yes, sex is a sin but abortion is too.

I had a very difficult time during my pregnancy; financially, things got very bad and emotionally, I was a wreck as the relationship between my child's father and I ended—*again*. But it was during that season that I truly experienced the power and provision of God in my life like I never had before. On October 6, 2011, I gave birth to the most precious gift, Christelle Rickaylia Garriques. I thank God every day for my support system—my awesome family, close friends, my church mates and my spiritual mothers who really loved me, encouraged me, and supported me throughout that season of my life.

Unfortunately, a few months after I had my baby, the flesh kept taking over so even after months of trying to live for God, I went back to my familiar lifestyle and "comfortable" relationship with my child's father.

True Conversion

Approaching my 26th birthday (August 2013), I just started to get very emotional *(I didn't realize it was conviction)*. After a failed engagement and constant relationship disappointments, the partying and sex just didn't seem as enticing anymore. I remember spending my birthday crying all day, eating cheesecake, drinking vodka and watching Twilight Saga. I had gotten to the point of complete brokenness so I started to beg God to help me to be a better person.

Everything I once thought was fun became awkward. Every time I had sex, I would be crying and I didn't know why. When I went to parties, I didn't enjoy myself and couldn't wait for them to be over. My friends would be asking me if I was okay because normally I would be dancing up a storm, but I truly wasn't interested anymore. Even the conversations with my friends felt weird, I felt horrible when

I gossiped or badmouth someone. I thought I was just getting older and didn't realize it was conviction at the time. All I knew was that something about me was changing and that sin was distasteful.

In November 2013, I finally made a pact with God that I would not have sex until I got married. At first, I thought it was impossible, but once I started researching how to live a pure life, I realized that it is possible. I listened to sermons and one day I came upon Heather Lindsey's blog (www.heatherllindsey.com) that truly touched my heart and encouraged me to stay celibate and live for God. My desire for God got even deeper once I got the courage to cut off the relationship with my child's father for good. My eyes were opened to how blessed and highly favored I am. I had achieved so much, and I knew it had nothing to do with me—it was ALL because God never stopped loving me. This time, I truly wanted to live a life that pleased God so I started pursuing Him like never before.

Brand New Me

As I yearned for a godly life, of course, the temptations came along with lots of trials and tests. I started to lose friends, had to get rid of many of my clothes, stopped partying and started to break soul ties from all the guys that I had sex with. I truly started to see that my worth was only found in Christ as the more I fed myself things of God, the more I started to hate the things God hated. I was constantly praying, reading my Bible, talking to other Christians, listening to YouTube sermons and reading many uplifting and religious blogs because I started to truly experience "true love." I was asked to be a part of my church's prayer team, and I felt so honored; for the first time, I felt that I was a true Christian. I got so much confidence to accept that I am a daughter of the King, born for a purpose, called to serve, and chosen for such a time as this. I got bolder talking about Christ to other people, making Facebook posts of what Christ freed me from, casting out demons in the name of Jesus, speaking in tongues, and I felt true passion and fire to share my testimony of transformation for God's glory. A brand new me was birthed.

Brand New Free

On Sunday, November 30, 2014, I was invited to Berean Church of God to preach my first sermon. Now, I never thought of myself as a preacher or even expected such a prestigious invitation, but I am passionate about sharing the gospel of Jesus Christ, and I was so honored. God is truly awesome! As I prayed and fasted about what my message should be about, I heard an Alicia Keys' song "Brand New Me" and even though it is not a gospel song, something ministered to me. I began to feel free… then I heard the Lord say, "Crystal, you have found a Brand New Free—Freedom in Me." This totally wrecked my heart.

Words from the Song by Alicia Keys:

It's been a while
I'm not who I was before
You look surprised
Your words don't burn me anymore
Been meanin' to tell ya
But I guess it's clear to see
Don't be mad
It's just a brand new kinda me
Can't be bad
I found a brand new kinda free

Ooh, it took a long, long road to get here
It took a brave, brave girl to try
I've taken one too many excuses, one too many lies
Don't be surprised, oh, said, you look surprised

Hey, if you were a friend
You'd wanna get to know me again
If you were worth the while

You'd be happy to see me smile
I'm not expecting sorry
I'm too busy finding myself
I got this
I found me, I found me, yeah

I don't need your opinion
I'm not waiting for your "OK"
I'll never be perfect,
But at least now I'm brave
I know my heart is open
I can finally breathe
Don't be mad
It's just a brand new kinda free

In the book of John Chapter 8 verses 31-36, Jesus spoke to the Jews about the Truth that can set them free. In verses 34-36 it states: "Jesus answered them, 'Most assuredly, I say to you, whoever commits sin is a slave of sin. And a slave does not abide in the house forever, but a son abides forever. Therefore, if the Son makes you free, you shall be free indeed.'"

Society tells us that we are "free" from slavery; we are free because we can do what we want, when we want, and how we want. The lost world convinces us that we can and should live anyway and that is freedom. I can confidently declare that life without Christ is a life of bondage and slavery under sin. I can stand boldly on the other side of true freedom with Jesus Christ and say, He has truly set me free— BRAND NEW FREE!

Many of us accept Christ because we hear a message and it makes us emotional. We feel guilty but not convicted. We feel like we need a free ticket to heaven in case we die. I know I did. I didn't truly want to live for Christ. I knew of God's grace, mercy, and forgiveness so I rode on that and used it as an excuse to live however I pleased. But Galatians 5:13 says we should not use our freedom in Christ as an excuse to live in sin. I wanted to be like the world, I wanted to fit in, I really didn't understand what holiness, righteousness or repentance was or what being a true Christian was about. The new Crystal hates sin, I don't profess to be sinless, that is far from the truth but the Holy Spirit who lives in me, convicts me when I sin, and I repent daily.

After reading the *Purpose Driven Life* by Rick Warren, the Lord ministered to my heart that I must share my story to help other young ladies. Honestly, confessing that I lived a double life and had an abortion was not something I wanted my parents to know, but Jesus set me free so I don't need to be ashamed. I still cringe at memories, but I know that was the foolish girl under the bondage of sin. Now, I have accepted that my life is not my own and my story will bring God glory.

I am a "chosen vessel" called to be a minister of the Gospel and servant of God. Instead of using politics to help people with natural needs, I now use the Gospel of Jesus Christ to offer them a greater life, a new life—a life of freedom that will save them from eternal damnation in hell and offer them eternal glory in paradise. This is the greatest gift I can share.

This is the beginning of what it means to be "Living a Royal Reality".

Chapter 2:

Accepting Your Identity

Royal Affirmation:

"I will not conform to the patterns of this world, but I will renew my mind in Christ." (Romans 12:2)

Do you really know who you are? Do you know your true identity? When you don't know who you truly are, you will easily sell yourself short and accept whatever is said about you. When you don't know your worth, you settle for less than your value. When you don't know your worth, you strive to find external means to make you feel valuable. You work hard to accomplish goals to get approval from others but these external means are temporary and unsustainable. Once you are disapproved of, your self-worth diminishes. This should not be.

To Live a Royal Reality, you must understand your true value and accept your identity, which is found in Christ Jesus. Your worth is not tied to what you do, what you possess, or what you have accomplished.

Our Eternal Father is a King and we are heirs of His kingdom. We have an inheritance of royalty as daughters of the King, chosen by God and loved dearly. We have been adopted into a kingdom with an unlimited source of power, provision, and freedom. We didn't earn this status as royalty. God chose us. Jesus signed a legal adoption through His blood. It is because of God's grace that we have been accepted with full legal status in the kingdom of God.

For example, if a family is interested in adopting a child, they go to the adoption agency and express their intent. The agency does the necessary checks to ensure the child will be in a safe environment and will be adequately provided for. The agency presents a contract to the parents giving them all the rights to the child. The child is now adopted into this new family. This means the adopted child now takes on the family's new identity and has the same access and inheritance as any biological child in that family.

The heavenly adoption is similar to the earthly adoption process. Galatians 3:26 says: "So in Christ Jesus you are all children of God through faith."

The blood of Jesus Christ is the contract that was signed on our behalf. Having placed faith in Christ, we are justified and accepted as sons and daughters of the King through the adoption process.

Unfortunately, many people say they've accepted Jesus Christ as their Savior but refuse to believe that they've been adopted into God's "royal" family and have access to His inheritance. They come at the door but are so fearful to come inside the kingdom, where there is power over sin, hope for the future, and abundant mercy. They look at their circumstances, past mistakes and allow their feelings to override what God has said about them in His word. 2 Corinthians 5:17 states, "This means that anyone who belongs to Christ has become a new person. The old life is gone; a new life has begun!"

This scripture tells us that our faith in Christ is our new identity. So, you are not identified by your feelings. You are not defined by what others think or say about you. You are not identified by your past mistakes or weaknesses. Also, John 1:12 states, "To all who received him, those believing in his name, he gave authority to become God's children"

Our new identity changes our relationship with God because we can now call Him, Abba Father. We can now confidently approach the King because we are now his daughters (Romans 8:15-16). This identity should change how we see ourselves, how we see the world and even more importantly, how the world sees us. We must accept and believe what God has said about us.

Today, you must choose to live your royal reality and accept that your worth, identity, confidence, and purpose is totally defined by our Creator.

Royalties, when we're secure in our relationship with Christ, we're no longer pressured by everybody else's expectations. God's love frees us to love others ungrudgingly. As we accept, we are now a part of God's royal family, as believers, we can strive to grow closer to the King. We extend grace, mercy, and forgiveness to each other as a reflection of the love God freely gives us.

Remember, your faith in Jesus Christ automatically qualifies you as royalty. It doesn't matter how many mistakes you've made or how many times you've failed. Christianity is truly not about us; it is all about Jesus Christ and what He has done to redeem us. But we are God's royal ambassadors on the earth. It is important to understand who God is and who He says we are so we can represent Him accurately.

The enemy would like nothing better than for you to believe the lies he says about you. Instead, you must believe the truth that Jesus shed His blood for all your sins and shame. God, the Father purchased us for the highest price—the blood of His Son. Grace is available to you. Grace is God's unmerited favor and His divine power that will help you to accept your identity.

If we second-guess our identity, everything else in our life will be easily compromised. Our identity (how we view ourselves), will determine our actions. If we see ourselves as victims, failures, and mistakes, we will live out this mindset in our daily lives. When unexpected situations happen, we will succumb to a defeated mindset and live in self-pity. In contrast, if we accept what God has said about us, that we are more than conquerors *(Romans 8:37)*, greatly loved *(Romans 5:8)*, His masterpiece *(Ephesians 2:10)* and that He is with us *(Psalms 118:6)*, *we can truly live a victorious life and walk in confidence that God has greater in store.*

Chapter 3:

Letting Go of The Past

Royal Affirmation:
"I am forgiven of all my sins; I am not condemned."
(Ephesians 1:7, Romans 8:1)

The first thing we need to accept is that we all have a past. I don't mean memories of the great achievements, lovely encounters or the unforgettable blessings we have experienced throughout our lives. Those are actually the memories worth holding on to. The moments of laughter, tears of joy and celebration are sometimes the things that keep us grounded in our times of despair.

We can't pretend that we don't have something or maybe even many things in our past that we are not proud of. We all have made decisions that we wish we could change; people have done or said things about us that have caused us great pain and hurt.

Personally, when I look back over my life; I cringed in embarrassment about many of the things I've done—dating so many guys, having unprotected sex, gossiping, stealing, constant lying, cheating, getting drunk and so many other distasteful acts. I got myself in so much trouble and hurt so many people. Sometimes, I do wish I could go back and do things differently. But in sin, we're so blinded by what appears to be pleasure until it's time to face the consequences. It's then that we realize the foolish decisions we've made.

Our reality won't change if we are stuck in the horrors of our past. Our pasts don't define us. We can actually choose to let go of the guilt. We can learn to forgive others and ourselves while believing that God can use even the most horrible experiences for His glory. That is the beginning of our healing process. For many of us, our most gruesome past experiences outweigh any of our good memories, and we are at the point where we wonder if life is even worth it any more. These self-condemning thoughts cripple us from truly becoming the royalty God has called us to be. But remember, Romans 8:1 states: "So now there is no condemnation for those who belong to Christ Jesus."

Royalty, because of the grace of God, you can choose to walk into your calling and purpose. Because of the grace of God, you can live by faith without fear of condemnation. I know you've experienced different levels of brokenness in your life. You may not have had any control over many of the things done to you including molestation, rape, abuse, lies told about you, loss of a loved one (parent, husband, child), divorce/separation, and false accusations. You are tempted to ask God why He allowed it to happen and what did you do to deserve such hurt or pain especially if He truly loves you as He said He does.

Believe me—I know the constant struggles of inadequacy and regret. I sometimes question if I'm even good enough to preach God's Word based on my past. I've felt rejection from friends and ex-lovers. I've experienced the crippling effects that come from fearing what people think about me or if I deserve God's goodness. I know the embarrassment of poverty and not being able to afford food to eat or having my car running out of gas on the road. I know the guilt of our past can cause us to get stuck and reject the royal inheritance that God has for us.

I know that letting go isn't easy, but it is possible. With Jesus Christ, it is more than possible (Philippians 4:13, Matthew 19:26). It won't happen overnight. It will take a daily decision to move forward and accept the promises of God.

I confess that even while writing this book, so much of my past resurfaced. I spent months trying to convince myself that it is the Devil who wanted me to share these personal secrets, but God reminded me that He has prepared me for such a time as this. As Revelation 12:11 lets us know, we have overcome him by the blood of the Lamb and the word of our testimony.

Two of the hardest past experiences for me to confess and let go of are the facts that I had an abortion and I was sexually molested. I didn't even tell my parents until I wrote this book because I had buried those memories with no plans of ever mentioning them again, but God wanted me to be transparent to the ladies reading this book. I know many women struggle with similar secrets and pain.

Honestly, I am only able to share them because I know with all my heart that God has set me free from the guilt and shame that I pretended didn't exist for many years.

I'm comforted when I read James 5:16, which says, *"Confess your faults one to another, and pray one for another, that you may be healed. The effectual fervent prayer of a righteous man avails much."*

As I said, some of our past experiences are consequences of the choices we make; whatever we sow, that is what we will reap (Galatians 6:7). Abortions, homosexuality, drug addictions, sexual promiscuity, strongholds of pornography, masturbation, and even prostitution are some of the realities we experience based on our poor choices. At the time, it might not have seemed like a choice because sin blinded us, but life always presents us with a good choice or bad choice. However most times, we choose the bad option because based on our temporary feelings it always seems easier at the time (Deuteronomy 30:19).

Unfortunately, these seemingly pleasurable choices have long-lasting effects that we have to deal with later on in our lives. These experiences are the ones we have to struggle with and eventually forgive ourselves for.

The other realities are the ones beyond our control. These painful experiences scar us significantly to the point of feeling like we can never forgive our perpetrators. These include sexual and physical abuse, abandonment issues by parents or spouses, poverty, betrayal by loved ones, rape, depression, being cheated on, sickness and rejection. We often compare our past to others believing that ours are far worse, which makes it harder to let go. The fact is, our struggles are incomparable. We don't understand the effect that something seemingly small can have on someone else because we all have been graced differently.

To Live A Royal Reality, we must let go of the past. We must be free from the bondage of hatred and bitterness or we will never be able to achieve our full potential in life. Someone once said, unforgiveness is like drinking poison and expecting the other person to die. We must start believing that we are worthy to be loved, accepted, and forgiven because God has already redeemed us. The only perfect man who walked the face of this earth, Jesus Christ, felt the ill effects of persecution from others, and He faced ridicule even though He was innocent. Just as remarkably, in the midst of it all, He said: "Lord forgive them for what they have done."

Ways we can let go:

1) **Believe and understand the power of forgiveness.** We always hear about forgiveness but many of us don't actually know how to forgive. Well, the best advice that I've gotten that I can testify to is prayer! Pray that God will help you forgive yourself; confess it all to Him (He knows anyway). Pray also for the offenders. It is very hard initially and you will be tempted to pray that God will strike them down (but don't)! Pray that they will repent. Pray that they won't hurt anyone else that way. Pray that God will forgive them. I promise the more you pray for them, the easier it will get.

If you want to cry, do so; scream if you must, journal, speak to a trusted friend or counselor but you must pray. Remember, no one can forgive for you. It is a personal choice to free yourself from the hurt and disappointment. I know it is hard, but we must try to extend the same mercy, grace, and forgiveness that Christ has extended to us to others (Matthew 6:15). Plus unforgiveness blocks your blessings—no one is worth that.

2) **Let go of the shame.** "Therefore, there is now no condemnation for those who are in Christ" (Romans 8:1). Know that we ALL make mistakes, but we are NOT a mistake. We sometimes do things consciously or unconsciously that may hurt others or ourselves. Or we are disobedient to God's commands and this can have a ripple effect because of the consequences we might have to deal with. The Word of God says, "If we confess our sins, He is faithful and just to forgive us" (1 John 1:19).

God doesn't hold anything against us after we have been forgiven. Why choose to dwell in self-pity and shame when Christ says, He has compassion for us? All our sins are as far as the east is to the west (Isaiah 1:18 and Psalm 103:12).

We have to continue reminding ourselves of our new identity in Christ and know that nothing we have done in our past can stop God from loving us or using us. There are many people in the Bible who had negative pasts, but God still used them. David committed adultery, Peter denied Christ, Paul persecuted the church, Noah got drunk, Rahab was a prostitute, Ruth was a widow and Moses disobeyed God. These men and women of God made mistakes and had messed up pasts, but God did not write them off—He won't hold it against you either. Nothing you have done can diminish your worth, hinder your purpose or decrease your royal inheritance.

3) **Stop keeping secrets with the Devil.** Until I was finally able to share my secrets with someone I trusted, I could not truly live my royal reality. Satan wants us to feel victimized and useless so he tries to constantly use our secrets to cripple us. He gives us self-defeating thoughts to plague our lives and make us hide behind the secrets and hurt. Hiding seems comfortable initially, but it is a lonely lifestyle to maintain, and it will sink us into deeper insecurity issues. With Jesus, we can come out of hiding.

There is no secret formula to let go of your past and move on, but we do have a choice. If we hang on to our past, we won't be able to truly receive all that God has in store for us.

Too many Christians are bound up in their past, as a result, they cannot fully live in their present. Before you can really start to move forward in your divine destiny with the Lord— you will first have to learn how to let your past go fully. Our past does not define our future! Ask for forgiveness from God, forgive others and forgive yourself.

"Blessed [fortunate, prosperous, favored by God] is he whose transgression is forgiven, And whose sin is covered." - Psalms 32:1

Chapter 4:

Being Apart of the Royal Family

Royal Affirmation:
"I am Royal, I am Holy, I am God's special daughter." (1 Peter 2:9)

Everyone knows the royal family of England (Queen Elizabeth, Prince Williams and so on…), but recently a new baby was born, Princess Charlotte. Now this baby girl was born just like every other baby in the world. Her mother carried her for nine months, she was delivered, she poops, she cries, she teethed and she does everything like any normal baby. But baby Charlotte, because of her family's royal status has the title of Princess. Since she was born like a normal baby, she obviously cannot simply act like royalty automatically. Instead, her title is now molding who she is destined to become and preparing her for her new role—A princess!

This means she has to learn to walk differently, talk differently, dress differently and eat differently. She can't hang around certain people because based on her title; she is now being "set apart" from the millions of other little girls around the world. But how does this happen?

Possibly, she has a code of conduct book, trainers or mentors, and family support. Her overall mindset now has to conform to fit her identity. For baby Charlotte, being a princess is more than just a title—it's a mindset.

This makes me think about the kingdom of God. Do you agree that God is the ultimate all-powerful King who reigns over the universe? If yes, that means if we are His children, then we are princes and princesses (royalties).

Galatians 3:26 states: "Through faith in Jesus Christ, we are children of The King." Romans 8:17 says: "We are children, then we are heirs of God (The King) and co-heirs with Christ (The Prince of Prince).

So why don't we believe that we are royalty? Why don't we behave like royalty? Why don't we speak like royalty? Why don't we accept this status?

I remember one day, I was singing the popular song by Lorde with the words "We'll never be royal." The Holy Spirit stopped me in my tracks and said, "Why are you singing that when the Word of God made it clear that we're daughters of the King, called to live like His royalty on this earth?"

God (The Father) has a massive kingdom, and He says once we are saved by the blood of Jesus Christ, we're royalty. At salvation, the believer becomes part of the most unique family—The Royal Family of God. As royalty, we can take charge of our circumstances, daily live in power and victory and refuse to be a slave to our past or walk in defeat.

At birth, we're mere creations of God. Sin separates us from having a relationship with God. We're mere slaves under sin. So none of us are automatically born as royalty. When we place our faith in Christ as Savior, we are born again into a new spiritual relationship with God, and we're adopted as His child. Through this adoption, we now have access and dominion over all the things that belong to The King. Through the adoption, as God's children, we now have rights and privileges of Sons and Daughters. (John 1:12, Galatians 4:1-2, Romans 8:15-17)

Now, some of you will hear that you are royalty and embrace this new awesome feeling of being a part of God's kingdom where everything is limitless and ALL things are possible. On the other hand, there are those of you who will want to reject this because you start looking at your "reality." You say: "I lost my job," "I lost my marriage," "I lost my self-worth," "I've lost my health" or "I just don't feel royal."

One thing we should know about royalty is that we can't step into the role without training. We have spent such a long time in the mental state of slavery that we have adopted the world's view. Consequently, even after we have been born-again and given the authority as conquerors, we still refuse to accept this.

Just like Princess Charlotte, we have to first accept this title of Royalty. We have to accept that as children of God, we're called to be "set apart" (Hebrews 10:10). That means we have to talk differently, think differently, and dress differently from the world. We use the guidelines found in the code of conduct (The Holy Bible), we need the mentor and trainer (HOLY SPIRIT), and we need the family support (The Church and our accountability partners).

Many people wear the "Christian" title but have not accepted the new Christ-like identity. This means our previous identity must die, and we now accept and conform to our new lifestyle. So, our mindsets must be renewed (Romans 12:2), and we must start to think pure thoughts (Philippians 4:8).

As kingdom citizens, we can rise above every circumstance. We can live in confidence, power, and boldness. We might not be able to choose certain situations that happen in our lives, but we are responsible for our own future and we can decide daily if we want to be victims or victors, failures or overcomers, defeated or more than conquerors! The Holy Spirit teaches us how to stand in authority no matter what troubles or difficulties come into our lives. It all begins with accepting that you are a member of the Royal Family of God; this changes how we see ourselves and how others will see us.

Kingdom living isn't about sitting back meekly to be defeated under the world's system. Claiming our inheritance has nothing to do with denominations or a particular church. It has everything to do with understanding our identity, which is grounded in the Lord of lords and Kings of kings. Success in life means learning not to walk in guilt and condemnation over our circumstances, which we have no control over. We are responsible for living a life that will affect others so that they will see the glory of the King in our lives.

We have to develop a kingdom mindset because it's the only way we can truly learn to walk in authority and reclaim our inheritance. Jesus made this statement:

"But seek the kingdom of God, and all these things shall be added to you. Do not fear, little flock, for it is your Father's good pleasure to give you the kingdom" – Luke 12:31-32

Ladies, you are ROYAL (princesses and queens) through the blood of Jesus Christ.

This is what determines your worth! Not what you have done or what others say about you. You're a part of the Royal Family and that can only change if we reject this title.

Being a part of the Royal Family of God assures me that someday my King will come and peace will reign. My royal inheritance here on earth will be nothing compared to what will be found in heaven.

Let's recite these promises until we know them and believe them:

- I am a Daughter of The King
- I am a Princess through God's Royal Family
- I am more precious than the lilies of the field
- I am a joint-heir with Christ
- I am a new creation
- I am under God's protective royalty—the enemy, the Devil cannot touch me
- I am a stranger to this world. Heaven is where my citizenship lies
- My body is the temple of the Holy Spirit who dwells in me

- I am redeemed and forgiven
- I am the apple of God's eye
- I am above and not beneath
- I am a blessed and highly favored
- I am being changed in the King's image
- I am capable and able to succeed
- I am on this earth to serve God and to serve others
- I am uniquely equipped and gifted for my mission
- My faith in God empowers me to face my fears
- I walk by faith and not by sight
- I can do all things through Christ who strengthens me

Chapter 5: Discovering Your Purpose

Royal Affirmation:
"I know God has plans to prosper me, to give me hope and a future." (Jeremiah 29:11)

Many people go through their lives looking for the next best thing to do. Feelings of discontentment bombard them because they wonder if their lives have any meaning. So many people believe that having more money will make them happy so they start seeking a new job; they think it's time to get another degree or try pursuing some "get-rich" scheme. Others believe that seeking a relationship or marriage will give them comfort; having a child will give them something to look forward to or acquiring material things (upgrading their car, buying a new house or acquiring more clothes) will make their lives happier. Unfortunately, the quest for more gets deeper, and they never recognize that this feeling of emptiness is caused by a God-void because no matter what they do, they aren't satisfied.

I remember always feeling like I had to be doing something. Whether it was school, taking on some project, or getting involved in a relationship. I always wanted more. Part of me always felt like something was missing so no matter how many parties I attended, relationships I got involved in or job promotions I got—I always felt like I needed more.

One day, I saw a post on Facebook that says, "There must be more to life than paying bills and dying." That challenged me so much. I started to question, could God put me on this earth for more? I had gotten to a place where I had done all that I could possibly do (relationships, friendships, career, house, car, baby, education, got baptized), but I knew something was still missing. That's how I started my purpose search…

I listened to many videos and read many blogs. Some of them spoke to my passions and gifts, a few mentioned seeking God to ask Him what my purpose is and I did, but it felt like God was hiding something from me.

When I finally stopped "seeking" my purpose and started to truly seek God and build a relationship with Him, I began to understand who I am in Him. Now I don't seek anything but Christ. I've found my purpose so I don't have to add meaningless activities in order to feel accomplished.

When you don't know who you are and what you have been called to do, you will continue to "do more" or search to find the next big thing in your life. For instance, the constant feeling of needing more money to make you happy in life will plague you so much. As you continue the quest for more, you see the years passing by and you are either stuck in one place or you have done so many things, but you still feel empty and unfulfilled.

We need to understand that we are created beings and this will give us a true picture that we cannot rely on ourselves to find out who we are or what we've been called to do. Keeping our eyes on ourselves will lead to pride, greed, idolatry, and eventually loss of hope.

> *"The Lord will fulfill his purpose for me, your steadfast love, O Lord endures forever. Do not forsake the work of your hands."*
> - *Psalm 138:8*

You will never know "who you are" outside of having a relationship with Jesus Christ.

Your relationship with God is what gives you access to God, The Creator, who loves you unconditionally. He did not create you by accident. Even before You were placed in your mothers womb, God appointed you with a purpose (Jeremiah 1:5).

We all have something to contribute in this life (John 17:4). If we seek God, He will show us exactly what He wants us to do and where we should serve in this life through our gifts, talents, and passions. Does this mean we can't have dreams or desires? No, I don't think so.

"Delight yourself in the Lord and He will give you the desires of your heart." — Psalm 37:4

I believe once our desire to please Him is far greater than us holding on to our own selfish dreams and plans, then we will begin to want what He desires for us.

For example, you may want a career, family, or even to live a comfortable life but the key is to delight yourself in Him. To delight in Him means to seek Him first and to love Him with all of our heart over anything else we may desire. Then and only then will He fulfill His promises to you and even exceed your expectations of what you think success will look like.

To live a royal reality, your life must be driven by purpose. Purpose is only found in Christ. If someone does not know God then how can they know their purpose? You might have an idea of what you are called to do but without Christ your desires are selfish and your motives are impure.

We are sinful by nature, in our thoughts and actions we are evil (Romans 3:23) and there is no good in any of us (Roman 3:12 and Mark 10:18).

We do things to feel better about ourselves, to mitigate the guilt we feel or enlarge our reputation with others! We can fool others and ourselves about our motives, but God knows our hearts (Jeremiah 17:9). Our motives to do anything must always be to please God, not us or other people (1 Thessalonians 2:4).

When we get saved, the Holy Spirit regenerates us and gives us power over sin. We have the freedom to obey Christ, and we are motivated by love rather than pleasing ourselves.

Many believers are still oblivious to the power they have access to in the kingdom. Some are still caught up in their worldly pursuits and haven't truly been "converted." James 4:4 says: "Anyone who chooses to be a friend of the world becomes an enemy of God." The world applauds sin and seeks pleasure through disobeying God. If we love God then our desire will be to please and obey Him above all other pleasures.

Purpose is the reason for existence. It is God's plan for our lives, without purpose life has no meaning. True success is found in fulfilling God's purpose for our lives (Acts 13:36).

Biblical Truths about Purpose:

1) God has a plan for your life and He had an intended result in mind when He created you. You are here on a personal assignment from God to bring glory to His kingdom in a unique way. God's plan for your life is the best version of you. (Jeremiah 29:11-13)

2) Your purpose includes helping and serving others. Jesus taught us that in order for us to be great, we should have a heart of a servant (Mark 10:43). The world defines greatness in terms of prestige, possessions, and power but that's contrary to what the Word of God teaches us. Know that whatever God has called you to do will glorify Him and impact others through service.

3) God works for the ultimate good of those in a relationship with Him, those who see His purpose as number one priority. This means no matter what you've gone through, God will use it for good. (Romans 8:28-29)

4) To accomplish the purpose of God in your life, God gives gifts that will help (Romans 12:4-8, 1 Corinthians 12). There are no major or minor gifts in the kingdom. God gives gifts to serve others and not to fulfill our own selfish agendas. To identify your gifts and talents, look at those things you are naturally good at and do with ease and excitement. These things will give you a sense of fulfillment and many times others are able to confirm them.

I suggest you read the book the *Purpose Driven Life (What on earth am I here for?)* by Rick Warren. This book truly helps to break down our callings, gifts and the impact we can make in the kingdom.

The Benefits of Knowing Your Purpose:

1) Purpose gives focus. When you know what God has called you to do and why you are here, then you won't go around trying to do everything, which can cause you to burn out. It will protect you from being distracted by other people's assignments.

2) Purpose gives confidence. When you discover your purpose, you will be persuaded to succeed and do the best

you can to serve God wholeheartedly by walking in obedience.

3) Purpose empowers you to persevere even through the midst of the "realities" of life. It keeps your focus on the greater that is ahead, creates a lasting joy, and sustains contentment. You won't have time to be worried about what others think about you or about comparing your journey with others.

In Living A Royal Reality, we accept that we're on this earth to make a contribution while becoming the best God has called us to be…

We do this by discovering God's purpose for our lives through:

- Accepting Jesus as your Lord and Savior
- Letting go of all we think we want to do, allowing Christ to lead us and fully surrendering.
- Seeking God with all our hearts to know His specific calling for our lives.

- Pray until our purpose is revealed. God may not necessarily show you everything but be obedient at every stage.
- Believe that God has forgiven you. Put your past behind you and know you are of more worth to God than you can imagine.
- You must also forgive others and release all of your offenders. Unforgiveness can hinder us from hearing God's voice.
- Take note of your gifts, talents, passions, and appreciate your experiences. Every gift helps to fulfill the purpose God has for your life.
- Never compare yourself to other people—purpose is not about having a ministry, a blog, preaching, singing in a choir—it's about glorifying God where you are with what you have.
- Understand your belief system as a child of God. Whatever you believe impacts the course of your life. Your thoughts generate your emotions and drive your actions, which determine your destiny. So start seeing yourself as God sees you.
- Now is the time to pursue your purpose. It's not just about doing "good" things but about fulfilling what God has placed you on this earth to do.

- Experience the heart of God. Know He is a loving and caring Father who strongly desires to bless His children. Sometimes, God is portrayed as a punisher who is looking for faults to condemn us but that's not the case. Even when He disciplines us, it's for our good and it's always to make us a better person and to become more like Him.
- Remember, your ultimate purpose in life is to glorify God and enjoy Him forever. You glorify God by fearing Him, obeying Him, worshipping Him, giving Him all your praises, keeping your eyes on eternity and getting to know Him intimately.

We are called to serve at whatever stage in life we are in. If what you are doing is not glorifying God, then it can't be your purpose. Apart from Him, we have no purpose.

Ladies, these are not formulas—finding purpose is not an overnight ritual. I am not an expert but over the past three years, I've been on this purpose journey with God. I've listened to many sermons and have read many books but the Holy Spirit has been the best teacher to me. My understanding of purpose is—becoming all you were to born to BE!

In other words, becoming the person God has created/called/destined you to be. This is a life-long process where our experiences, passions, gifts, and assignments all align to radiate who God is. It really has nothing to do with us, He uses us to show who He is to others. Through this, we are able to live the best life possible.

Many people think purpose is about "doing" things. The "doing" part is just an expression of your purpose. So the ministry, the books, the singing, dancing or evangelizing and all the things we do in the kingdom are not your purpose, per say, but who you are (that is who God created you to be) is expressed through these things. Understand that being a preacher, worship leader, speaker, lawyer, doctor, stay-at-home mom, entrepreneur or whatever else God has called you to do and contribute to His kingdom, do not define who you are. If you know this, then you won't be caught up in what you are necessarily "doing" but what you bring to what you do—that is what truly matters.

Discovering "who you are" leads to a powerful and transforming life. It is my deepest desire and prayer that you realize that you can be content in this life. You can overcome all your "realities" and use these tests as testimonies of God's faithfulness. If you seek God for who He is and not get caught up in what He can do for you, it is the beginning of joy and peace in your life. Know that you are a missing puzzle in the kingdom. There is something that you should be doing but don't let this be your focus. Remember, anything you chase over God is an idol. Trust that God will guide you. Read His Word and listen with expectations. Keep your eyes on Him!

Chapter 6:

Broken for His Glory

Royal Affirmation:

"I am more than a conqueror through Christ who loves me and gave Himself for me." (Romans 8:37)

Many of us spend so much time on social media portraying a façade, posting flawless pictures, saying the proper things and getting hundreds of "likes" on our photos. It appears that we have it all together when in reality we truly DON'T.

We all have a different story. We all face different fears, insecurities and sometimes were totally broken. We go through times where the pain is so devastating that we question God and start doubting that He has a plan or even a purpose for our lives.

God will not allow the pain that you've experienced throughout your life to go to waste. We are broken for God's glory. God wants to use our pain, brokenness, and our weakness to prove His strength and that He can still work miracles in our lives. In the brokenness of our lives, God is most glorified.

One of the hardest times in my life was when I got pregnant. Things were rough for me financially and some of the people who I thought would be there for me totally deserted me and treated me harshly, including my child's father.

Many wouldn't even imagine the level of brokenness I went through in that season. My reputation was severely tarnished with so many rumors circulating about me in my community. My living conditions were not very comfortable, and I even started to worry if it would be appropriate for a newborn baby; plus, I was an emotional wreck.

During that time, my faith grew in God like never before. I truly had to learn to trust in His promises and that He is my provider, my deliverer and the source of my strength. Despite the hardship I faced, I am so thankful for my church family that was very supportive and never stopped praying for me. I had some faithful friends who really tried to encourage me and I had my family who supported me and loved me endlessly, which helped me to press through that season.

Now here I am four years later, writing this book to encourage you that whatever you are going through is temporary and you can make it. During the broken season, I implore you to pray without ceasing, journal, cry, or scream. Do whatever it takes to relieve those feelings and fight the emotions. Don't bottle them up.

Romans 8:28 states "But we do know that all things work together for good to those who love God, to those who are called according to His purpose." I can undoubtedly say that God has truly used my pain to strengthen me. He also continues to use my testimonies to bless many people as I get to share my struggles to help someone get through theirs. It's all totally worth it. It was during the broken seasons of my life where I've continuously witnessed God's faithfulness in my life. God allows the pain to prepare us for purpose, destiny, and for His glory. It's during these seasons that we realize how God is really strong in our weakness.

"But he said to me, 'My grace is sufficient for you, for my power is made perfect in weakness." Therefore, I will boast all the more gladly about my weaknesses so that Christ's power may rest on me. That is why, for Christ's sake, I delight in weaknesses, in insults, in hardships, in persecutions, in difficulties. For when I am weak, then I am strong." - 2 Corinthians 12:9-10

In these intense moments of our trials and tribulations we must decide that we will press through and not give up. We must trust that God will never leave us, nor forsake us. We should cast our cares on Him because He truly does care for us.

Remember your greatest ministry is birthed through pain. Your pain won't be wasted. Don't hold back and hide it. There is nothing for you to be embarrassed about—as Solomon says "there is nothing new under the sun" *(Ecclesiastes 1:9)*. Believe it or not, there is someone going through the same struggle you are going through, or even worse. Be honest with God, yourself, and other people you trust. Your brokenness will help someone if you share it and God will be glorified through it all. God cares very deeply for you. No matter how bad things may seem, He is in control!

Chapter 7:

Beauty in the Eyes of the Creator

Royal Affirmation:
"I am fearfully and wonderfully made."
(Psalms 139:14)

There is a popular phrase that we grow up hearing and accepting, "Beauty is in the eyes of the beholder." This phrase tells us that others determine our beauty based on their opinion of us and that they decide who and what is beautiful. Today, I want to tell you, that is a lie from the pit of hell!

I want you to replace that idea with God's truth and renew your mind to know that "Beauty is in the eyes of the Creator." That means, what society says or feels does not determine how beautiful you are, but God who created us and made us in His image and likeness has already defined that you are fearfully and wonderfully made (Ps. 139:14). Let me ask you—when you look in the mirror what do you see? Are you thankful for God's creation or critical of His handiwork?

Growing up, I was not considered the "prettiest" girl according to society's standards. I was short, very skinny, my face was filled with acne, nappy hair, and I was dark-skinned. I was not able to get the guys attention because their definition of beauty was long hair, light skin, financial status, and popularity. As I got older, I started to succumb to the pressures of what was expected of me to get attention from men. I dressed in skimpy outfits, wore padded bras and at one point, I even started to "bleach" my skin.

When I rededicated my life to the Lord, He began to strip me of my shallowness and false confidence. In 2015, God told me to stop wearing extensions, no more tips on my nails and get rid of many of my outfits. Honestly—it was really hard. I had to learn to appreciate the beautiful me that God has created me to be.

Women of all ages, ethnic groups, nationalities, social status and various backgrounds ALL suffer from the "reality" of trying to look beautiful to fit into society's standards. We spend time and energy criticizing and analyzing our facial features, body, and hair. Some women feed themselves false definitions of beauty gained by popularity on social media, entering pageants or attention given by the opposite sex. Many times, pride and ego take over and they'll start belittling others to make themselves feel better. Other women struggle with the opposite, where they can't even look in the mirror most times because what they see doesn't measure up with the images on television and in the magazines. What category are you in?

What Beauty Isn't

Sometimes to appear beautiful, women will bleach their skin because they think "black is not good enough." Some women have tattoos and piercings all over their body, always wear extensions, starve themselves to lose weight, get plastic surgery and liposuction, go to tanning booths, get breast implants, constantly put on make up and get extreme makeovers without wanting to admit that the reason for doing these things is to gain popularity, acceptance, and attention from men. These things are done to seek approval and gain sex appeal. In the process, we compromise our worth in order to fit into the world's definition of beauty.

What Beauty Is

True beauty radiates from the inside; it is a heart that delights in the Word. This beauty is not external because we know that everything external is temporary. As we age, our features change and we may not be as confident if we have not accepted God's definition of beauty.

Have you ever met anyone who appears "pretty" but they have a stinky attitude? I'm sure we all have. We can try accessorizing or adorning our external features but if our hearts are impure, our thoughts are evil and our souls belong to Satan, the fact is, we will be far less attractive. We must first accept that we are made unique. The space between your teeth, the "plug" nose, the "buff" teeth; the glasses you wear, the acne or scar on your face, your dark or light skin, the thickness of your bones or skinniness are what make you unique. Our God is a God of variety, and our physical appearance represents His creativity.

You are beautiful because God made you beautiful—even without "enhancements" you are beautiful. This beauty cannot radiate if our heart is not pure. It's good to love yourself but even that is a vain approach to beauty because the battle of trying to accept yourself can lead to self-defeat or pride.

Beauty is a heart motivated by a love for God. We must also love our neighbor and have a desire to be like Christ. Imagine if we truly started seeing ourselves as God sees us, beautiful, unique, special, set-apart, and loved—wouldn't we be able to accept each other and appreciate variety? (1 Peter 3:3-4, Proverbs 31:30). We need to accept that the images portrayed in the media are false. Many celebrities spend thousands of dollars on professional hair, dresses, makeup artists, image consultants, and airbrushed photos to hide their true self. The cellulite and stretch marks are cancelled by some makeup and the magic of Photoshop.

Only when we are born-again, and we receive the Holy Spirit will we be able to radiate feminine beauty, discover purpose, emulate true worth, identity, motivation, esteem, and confidence. When we exchange self-promotion for godly humility, that's when we will truly learn to cultivate incorruptible beauty that comes from Christ.

The illusion of a coke bottle figure, Botox, make-up tricks to narrow the look of the nose, flatten the lips, narrow the face and brush away wrinkles are all a façade. These things are used to cover up low self-esteem, drug addiction, body dissatisfaction, self-hatred, alcoholism, and depression. These are the "realities" that many women have today.

Living a Royal Reality means accepting that your uniqueness is needed in the world. It means being honest, caring for others, being respectful, and confident so that when you draw out the beauty from the inside, it will radiate externally, while drawing the right people to you. So the next time you are quick to criticize another woman about her appearance (she is too fat, too slim, she can't dress, she's ugly…), remember, you are not only criticizing her, but you are also criticizing God's creation.

Chapter 8:

God ~~Self~~ Confidence

Royal Affirmation"
"I have power and authority in the name of Jesus."
(Luke 10:19)

In our society today, there is a new era of life coaches and motivational speakers rising up. Their main idea is to build self-confidence, self-esteem, and self-worth because the struggle with insecurity is so real.

As women, many of us have struggled with these issues. We may lack confidence because we don't fit in with the "popular girls," we can't afford to wear certain hairstyles or outfits, and we don't feel as beautiful as the ladies on the magazine covers, therefore, our worth has been severely tainted.

The fact is, society has taught us that our worth, esteem, and confidence extends from our appearance, skills, accomplishments, status, and financial resources. The danger of lacking confidence is that it will prevent you from living a fulfilling life and accomplishing your God-given destiny. The Devil has used our lack of knowledge of our identity, worth, and confidence to stop us from being effective in the kingdom. You can see the results manifesting as depression, confusion, fear, indecisiveness, pride, and overall lack of favor. As royalties, we must be conscious of the enemy's tactics. All over the Scriptures, we realize that our worth, confidence, and identity really have nothing to do with us, but everything about us has been dictated by God.

For many years, I was fooled by the constant promotion of self-confidence, self-worth, finding beauty from within, discovering purpose through our passions/talents, self-identity, self-motivation, self-esteem, and the continuous fallacy of promotion of "self." Because many of us continue to compare ourselves to the Victoria Secret's models and celebrities, we are always struggling with insecurities and the constant feeling inadequacy plagues us when we don't match up to society's expectations.

Since I've truly developed a relationship with Christ, my eyes have been opened to the level of deceit by these self-promoting messages. I realized that my confidence is found through Him, my esteem is built on Him and He determines my worth.

If I have low self-esteem, I know that the root is pride because I am searching to find comfort in people. If I have low self-confidence that means I don't trust God and His ability to accomplish His will through me. If I have low self-worth then I am rejecting what Jesus did on the cross for me.

Many women suffer from low self-image. This is how they see themselves or how they believe others see them. From childhood, Satan starts to plant seeds of worthlessness, insecurity, and inadequacy in our minds. He uses people to tell us we are not good enough, pretty enough, rich enough, and we, unfortunately, live defeated lives because we believe his lies.

Satan is an identity thief! He tries to rob us of our earthly and heavenly legacy. Confidence starts from the inside and radiates on the outside. In order for you to be truly confident, you have to develop an authentic relationship with God. The root of our confidence issues is based on fear. *1John 4:18* states that God's perfect love casts out all fear. This is why you must build a foundation grounded by His love. Confidence is hearing God's Word and believing what He has said about you.

Satan tries to convince us that God does not love us and if He did, He wouldn't allow so many things to happen to us. We have to reject this lie! We have to confess with our mouths and believe with our hearts that God truly loves us, and He has fashioned us in His likeness. Spend time with God; fall in love with the lover of your soul. Start giving God thanks for how He made you (Psalm139:13-15). So your big nose, gap teeth, nappy hair, short stature, skinniness, whatever it is… is beautiful and when you focus on God, you will accept that you are made in His image. Flaws and all, you are completely loved (Isaiah 54:10), you are completely accepted (Titus 3:7), and you're extremely valuable (1 Corinthians 7:23). Know you cannot earn His love; you just have to receive it.

Seven (7) ways to boost your confidence:

1. Spend time giving God heartfelt praise and focus on Him. The more you hear the Word of God, the more your faith will develop. The more your faith is developed, the more confident you will become in who God has truly called you to be.

2. Practice speaking positive and faith-filled words over your life. You cannot dwell in negativity and expect a positive life. Consistently declare the positive affirmations given through God's promises.

3. Practice loving yourself. Care for your feelings like you would a friend. Empathize and go easy on yourself when you make a mistake. Learn to laugh at yourself.

4. Stop comparing yourself to others. God made you unique and you can only be the best version of you.

5. Stop criticizing or thinking bad things about others. If you do, you can ensure others are criticizing you too.

6. Look your best. It's not about wearing designer clothes, but it's about being comfortable in what you can afford. Fix yourself up, comb your hair and smile—that's your best makeup.

7. Laugh, have fun, and hang out with positive people. Get the support of trusted friends or company to talk to when you feel down.

In order for us to do what God has called us to do, we need to be confident and have faith that the best years of our lives are ahead of us.

Chapter 9: Overcoming Inadequacy

Royal Affirmation:
"I am competent. I am qualified. I am enough through Jesus Christ." (2 Corinthians 3:5)

It was three months before the 1st She's Royal Empowerment Conference, I was excited because in 2014, the Lord told me that He wanted me to have a conference where women could come together to empower one another and worship Him. The planning part was fun and fairly easy but the Lord placed on my heart to be the keynote speaker on the first night of the conference.

Feelings of inadequacy started to bombard me and when I got the final poster/flyer for the conference with my photograph on it, I panicked! I panicked because this was real—I was expected to speak at a conference with 100 women, and I felt I was not good enough to do it. Questions started to race through my mind: "What do I know about speaking? I am not eloquent. I am not popular. There are so many other women far more qualified to speak than I am. I just can't do it Lord".

As women, I believe at one point or another, we all struggle with feelings of inadequacy. According to *Dictionary.com*, inadequacy means "not being good enough or lack of quality or quantity required." In other words, you don't believe you have what it takes to succeed at something. Inadequacy can lead to low self-worth, feeling incompetent, powerlessness, shame, and even depression. The feelings of inadequacy can be triggered by the belief that you lack money, lack support, lack ability, comparing yourself with others who you think are more successful than you are, lack of qualification, lack of beauty or power. As I prayed and started to truly express how I felt to God, He spoke to me and said, "You are enough!"

We have to come to the realization that there is always someone smarter, prettier, more eloquent, wealthier, and more popular than we are, so if we look to the world, we will always feel inadequate. But if we keep our eyes on the Lord, we will be reminded that Jesus Christ has made us capable, competent, and complete! Let's ask ourselves whose approval we are after. Why do we think we need to impress others? Are we seeking to please everyone else instead of God?

Honestly, at the end of the day, if we're not living our own truth and doing things that are aligned with our calling and identity, we will always be unfulfilled and empty. We have to remember that the enemy prowls around like a roaring lion seeking whom he can devour (1 Peter 5:8) and he is seeking to kill, steal, and destroy your future (John 10:10). The mind is the battlefield. This is where he first seeks to attack and if he can conquer our thoughts then we will easily fall into his trap of deception.

This is why we are encouraged to always have our armor, which includes the helmet of salvation (Ephesians 6:17). The helmet protects us from Satan's fiery darts so they do not lodge in our thoughts, and we can take every thought captive to the obedience of Christ (2 Corinthians 10:5). The Word of God says to renew our minds (Romans 12:2), fix our eyes on things above (Colossians 3:2), and focus on noble things (Philippians 4:8) because every temptation, struggle, and fall begins with our thoughts.

Royalty—You are enough! You're enough not because you have a degree, you dress well, you won a pageant, have your own car or are married—you are enough because Jesus' power is within you. Greater is He (Christ) that is in you than He that is in the world, you can do ALL (not some) things through Christ who gives you the strength. Take your eyes off of the situation, world, and yourself. Put your focus on Christ who has great plans for your life (Isaiah 55:8, Proverbs 16:6, Jeremiah 29:11).

Here are some tips to help you overcome inadequacy:

1. Remind yourself that you are not who other people think or say you are. Your identity is found in who God says you are.

2. Remind yourself that everyone makes mistakes and everyone has weaknesses. In reality, we have no idea what really goes on in most people's lives and minds, no matter how successful, happy and confident they look, so don't compare—you don't know the full story.

3. Remind yourself that every day is a choice. We can choose to believe the worst about ourselves or choose to believe we are good enough.

4. Remember, we are not defined by our feelings. Feelings are temporary. They are not facts. Just because we feel a certain way doesn't mean we are that way.

5. Remind yourself that you don't need everyone else's approval. Keep friends who appreciate you, encourage you, and know your worth. Even though you have these people in your life, you have to become your biggest cheerleader. If God has given you dreams, go for them. Don't let the opinions of the crowd stop you from being who you are called to be and doing what you are meant to do.

When you feel inadequate, remember God says you are CHOSEN (Isaiah 43:40) when you feel afraid, remember God says you are REDEEMED (Isaiah 43:1). When you feel insecure, remember God says you are SECURE (Deuteronomy 33:12). When you feel worthless, remember God says you are CALLED (1 Peter 2:9).

Life can be full of disappointments. Life can be unfair. But we cannot sit and feel sorry for ourselves just because we don't think we have it as good as someone else. We need to make the best out of what we are given. This is what living a royal reality is about; not pretending our lives are perfect but trusting that despite the circumstances, we can smile because His strength is made perfect in our weakness. We are enough in Him!

Chapter 10: Develop a Zero Tolerance for Excuses

Royal Affirmation:

"My tongue has the power to change things for the better." (James 3:2-5)

Failure is inevitable in life. At one point in each of our lives, we will fail at something but this is not an excuse to walk away or give up. The fact is—in order for us to live a royal reality; we must develop a zero tolerance for excuses.

If you desire to achieve anything worthwhile in life, you must make a decision today to not accept excuses. Excuses are the currency of poverty and (insecurity). Excuses lead to a life of emptiness. If you are proficient in making excuses, the fact is, you will reap abundant regret.

You must make the decision to take action and make things happen. Life is never easy, things will happen that you don't have control over but do not just sit back and accept defeat. Take responsibility for your actions and fight the urge to explain why you didn't do what you were supposed to do.

Even if you did the best you could with what you had and that failed, don't just sit back and accept defeat. Truth is, while you are busy making excuses, others are making a difference.

I remember attending a friend's father's funeral; he had a few successful businesses and was known as one of the top merchants in Downtown, Kingston. That weekend, the t-shirt business I started was just not going how I thought it would. I literally gave up and started finding all the excuses in the world.

I knew nothing about owning a business, the supplier robbed me, and I had to pay back loans for a business that had failed. I thought my excuses could validate my actions until I attended my friend's father's funeral that weekend. As his son read the eulogy, he shared that his father failed in his business ventures 18 times but each time, he gave it one more chance. The fact is, success, glamour, and accomplishments are all a product of hard work, tears, sacrifices, and persistence. Giving up is never an option. Excuses are never an option. Dare to be a woman of actions and results.

Ladies, find a way to do it. Losers find excuses for giving up. Proverbs 10:4 states "Poor is he who works with a negligent hand, But the hand of the diligent makes rich"

We cannot accept defeat or make excuses. Take your dreams and plans and execute them proficiently—take it seriously.

"I can do everything through Christ, who gives me strength."
- Philippians 4:13

It's so easy to say "I was born poor so I will never get a college degree," "no one in my family ever finished high school so I won't either," "I don't know anything about preaching so I cannot share the gospel," "I was raped so I will never be a role model," Our circumstances don't define us. Excuses cannot be tolerated, no matter how "true" they appear. The power we receive in union with Christ is sufficient to do His will and to overcome every challenge that may arise. So Royalty, no more excuses. No matter what it is. Just do it!

Chapter 11: Choose Your Friends Wisely

Royal Affirmation:

"I will keep friends who will stick closer than a sister." (Proverbs 18:24)

There's a saying: "If you want to know who your real friends are, pretend like you're dead." But I don't agree with that because when you're dead, people will pretend that all is well. So let me tell you a better way—if you really want to know your true friends "Give your life to Christ"." Seriously! Once you become a Christian that's when you see the true test of friendship and those who will truly be loyal to you.

Many times, our "friendships" are based on situations, familiarity or common interests. We believe they are sincere until a life-change occurs and we realize many of these people truly don't have our best interest at heart. So ask yourself: "Will they still be your friend when you no longer want to gossip or talk negatively about others? Will they still be your friend when you no longer go clubbing or partying? Will they still be your friend if you don't have stuff to give? Will they accept the true you? These are questions you need to ask yourself as you evaluate the friends in your life.

Let me confess, before Christ, I had many friends. I was one of those people who would have 10 bridesmaids at their wedding because I loved all my friends, and I always tried to be loyal. I'm very sociable, so at work, I have friends, party friends, and even friends from my kindergarten years. I didn't understand the importance of seasons and purpose in regards to true friendships until I came into Christ.

First, we should understand that relationships are important. God created us as relational beings. Romans 12:5 says: "Since we are all one body in Christ, we belong to each other, and each of us needs all the others." So, no matter what age or stage we are in life, we find ourselves looking for friends, connections, and acceptance. The Bible says if we surround ourselves with bad company, our morals will be corrupted (1 Corinthians 15:33), therefore, it is essential that we evaluate and filter our friendships because they can either help make us or break us.

It is so important that we surround ourselves with the right people. To live a royal reality, we must come to the realization that friends will come and go with the passing of time. Some friends will be for a lifetime and others will only be for a season. Some friends will always have a special place in our hearts even though their love for us may have changed or was dismissed. And that's okay! We must accept that this is a part of the journey of life. Sometimes, it can be heartbreaking and disappointing but understand that God knows what's best.

We live in a world where envy, jealousy, and malice are very prevalent, so no matter how hard you try, you cannot be everybody's friend. This is why knowing your purpose in life is so important because if your friends are not pushing you towards Christ or encouraging you to be the best God has called you to be then maybe, it's time to break ties. You cannot become who you're destined to be if you keep hanging around people who are jealous of the person you are becoming.

Good friendships take cultivation, time to build, a deep connection and require commitment. Earthly friendships can be complicated because we are imperfect human beings. But Proverbs 18:24 says, "A man of many companions may come to ruin, but there is a friend that sticks closer than a brother." Therefore, you don't need many friends but a few loyal ones will add value to your journey in life.

Chapter 12:

Pursuit of Purity

Royal Affirmation:
"I will think on things that are true, noble, right, pure, lovely, and admirable." (Philippians 4:8)

One of our biggest issues in this life as women, is men! We cannot deny that as young as possibly nine (9) years old many of us start to develop a certain level of attraction to the opposite sex. Once we hit puberty, we get so self-conscious about our appearance (how we dress or comb our hair) and our physical bodies (breast size, hip size or if we are pretty enough). We get butterflies when a certain guy passes our way; we want his attention but don't want him to know we want his attention. We start to write little love notes in our books, scribble hearts with his name on it and even start daydreaming about marrying and having a family. It all starts with these innocent thoughts.

Honestly, we weren't thinking about having sex. What consumed our thoughts are love, affection, and attention.

Unfortunately, many of us were not taught how to deal with these emotions especially when our sexual desires begin to heighten. Many parents don't talk to their children about sex and if they do, it's just to scare them to not get pregnant. Even in churches, young people are not taught about true purity, it's mostly hell messages to scare us again. These techniques rarely work, because the music we listen to teach us otherwise, the movies we watch don't help these desires and overall, it's the culture that dictates how we view sex, which is totally contrary to how God designed it.

Unfortunately, I got caught in the world's view of sex. I wasn't seeking love from men per say but the rousing emotions and feelings led me to be exposed to sexual immorality at a young age. Now, to many people, sixteen years old is not too young to have sex, but we know any age outside of marriage is totally wrong in God's eyes and that's the standard we will be judged by.

Purity is far more than just having sex. Frankly speaking, many might not have gone the full way of having sex, but they have been kissing, fondling, fingering, and even engaging in oral sex to avoid penetration so they can still appear to be virgins.

As Royalties, we must understand that pursuing purity is not only a choice, but it is a lifestyle. Purity is about the state of the heart, not just our actions. You can remain a virgin or celibate until marriage and still be impure in God's eyes.

"How blessed are those who are pure in heart, because it is they who will see God!" - Matthew 5:8

When we hear words like "holy," "sanctified," "righteous" and "purity," many of us cringe. I know even when I got baptized in 2009; I would never put my name in a sentence with those words. To be honest, when I thought about my background, it would be an insult to describe myself that way. I was in church on Sundays, attended the prayer meetings, posting scriptures online and trying to do devotions, but I knew nothing about being called to holiness (1 Peter 1:16), that it was God's will for me to be sanctified (1 Thessalonians 4:3) or I was supposed to live in purity (Psalm 119:9). These things weren't taught to me in church. Yes, I knew that the Bible said do not have sex before marriage but honestly for me, that wasn't enough reason not to. Plus, I had already been exposed to sex, so I constantly asked these questions: Was I truly expected to stop? Is it even possible to stop? And if it was possible, why are so many Christians still having sex outside of marriage? Suppose I never get married, does that mean I won't have sex again? There aren't many men in church so how will I even find a husband? Suppose I wait until marriage and then the sex is bad?

Since I couldn't get any comforting answers to these questions, I continued to fornicate even after I got baptized. Then, after my daughter turned two years old, the conviction on my heart became stronger than ever. Even though I still could not answer many of these questions, I had experienced so many disappointments from men so I decided to abstain until after marriage. The appetite for the Word of God got so deep; I spent hours researching the answers to these questions. I had read many blogs and listened to many sermons that gave me faith that if I trusted God to choose my husband then He would work it all out.

Romans 10:17 says, "Faith comes by hearing, and hearing by the Word of God." This has proven to be true. The more I spent time with God, He started to show me that I'm worth far more than being a girlfriend, baby mother, "ride or die chic" mistress or friend with benefits. He has called me to be a wife and I should not settle.

As I said before, purity is far more than just not having sex. The process of purity includes constantly renewing the mind, godly conduct, becoming more like Christ and of course, fleeing from sexual immorality. Purity is reflected in how we carry ourselves (dressing modestly and our mannerisms). It's reflected in how we treat the opposite sex (being flirty or causing lust) and even how we speak (gossip, expletives and type of conversation we entertain).

To today's society purity sounds like being in quarantine or living in a monastery where you have to wear long overalls and pray 24 hours a day to avoid sin. When we accept that we are set apart by God (when we accept His gift of salvation), then pursuing purity becomes natural. You will not become instantly pure but daily it will get easier as we grow more in Him.

I'm daily asked, even by Christians, if I really believe it's even possible or really necessary to live a life of purity before God. Ladies, it is very necessary! Purity is important to Christ so it should be important to us.

Purity cannot be achieved by our own strength. When we pursue purity, we have to pursue God and allow His power to manifest in us so that His name will be glorified. It takes a supernatural power to not be swayed by the songs, movies, cartoons and books we read or even peer pressure. The Holy Spirit who lives in us will empower us to pursue a lifestyle of purity.

"The Spirit of God, who raised Jesus from the dead, lives in you. And just as God raised Christ Jesus from the dead, he will give life to your mortal bodies by this same Spirit living within you." - Romans 8:11

Why Pursue Purity?

When we pursue purity we're shielded from condemnation, feelings of unworthiness, fear, doubt, and insecurities. Purity sets the right foundation in our relationships. Many times, we are blinded by lust, thinking its love because we got tangled up in sexual immorality.

Purity protects us from emotional heartbreaks, sexually transmitted diseases, unwanted pregnancies, and soul ties. It protects our mind, emotions, and future.

How can we stay sexually pure?

1) Get in God's Word daily – Psalm 119:9 says, "How can a young person stay on the path of purity? By living according to your word." If we don't know what the Word of God says then we will be swayed by what society says. So it is essential that we renew our minds daily to contradict everything that we have been taught about sex.

2) Forgive yourself – Psalms 103:12 says: "As far as the east is from the west, so far has He removed our transgressions from us." Sometimes, we try to torture ourselves because of our previous choices, but we have to learn to forgive ourselves. Once we are saved, we are new creatures in Christ.

3) Socialize with other believers – Bad company corrupts good morals (1 Corinthians 15:33). Whether we want to admit it or not, our friends have a lot of influence on the decisions we make daily. We all want that sense of belonging, so we easily compromise to fit in. We should surround ourselves with like-minded people who will help keep us accountable.

4) If you're dating, set boundaries early in the relationship. Ensure that both of you are on the same page about living pure. This is why it is so important that we date believers, 2 Corinthians 6:14 says: "Do not be unequally yoked with unbelievers." Forming relationships with unbelievers will weaken your Christian commitment or standards because you will find yourself compromising to make the other person comfortable.

5) If you're married, avoid entertaining certain relationships with the opposite sex. Cheating doesn't happen overnight, it normally happens by getting close to someone over a period of time and letting your guard down. Avoid conversations that your spouse wouldn't approve of. Women who are married also struggle with impurity, so guard your thoughts and heart.

6) Fight back against the enemy's lies – John 10:10 says: "Satan comes to steal, kill and destroy." We have to realize that our flesh will always lead us astray because we are born in sin. We also have an adversary to deal with, who tries to plant seeds of doubt about God's plan for our lives. He will tell you that you won't ever get married, he will use your past mistakes against you, he will send distractions and counterfeit men to have you take your eyes off of God. We have to reject these lies!

7) Pray- Pray without ceasing—give thanks and worship. Our lifestyle of purity can only be maintained through constant prayer and worship to God. The more focused we are on Him, the less time we have to focus on our own desires.

Royalties, let us truly understand that our bodies belong to God. So we cannot do with our bodies as we please. Sexual sins are forbidden because our bodies are temples of the Lord.

"Do you not know that you[a] are God's temple and that God's Spirit dwells in you? If anyone destroys God's temple, God will destroy him. For God's temple is holy, and you are that temple."
- 1 Corinthians 3:16-17

1 Corinthians 6:9-10 says: "Do you not know that the wicked will not inherit the kingdom of God? Do not be deceived: Neither the sexually immoral nor idolaters nor adulterers nor male prostitutes nor homosexual offenders nor thieves nor the greedy nor drunkards nor slanderers nor swindlers will inherit the kingdom of God." When we commit sexual sins, we sin both against God and our body. This is why when we have sex it leaves such a permanent mark. God has reserved the pleasure of sex for the union of marriage. It doesn't matter how much society tries to convince us that living pure is not possible, nor does it matter how many other Christians are doing it. God will never change His mind. If He says it is wrong then, it is still wrong now.

Again, abstaining from sex is one thing but remember, purity includes the substance of our thoughts, our hearts and even our motives for doing what we do. Purity is not a religious thing to try and earn God's love. It's not a ritual to stop you from "enjoying life." It is a choice we make to protect our minds, bodies, hearts and future. It's a choice to live a Royal Reality.

Chapter 13:

Act Like a Lady, Think Like Jesus

Royal Affirmation:
"I have the mind of Christ, therefore, I will act in a way consistent to His actions." (1 Corinthians 2:16)

In our society, we have a lot of women who are considered beautiful, confident, and successful. These women are accomplished according to the world's standards and many of our young people are drawn to this definition of "success." As royalties, we cannot let these women faze us. God's standard for success is very different. These women are not living their true purpose and potential because without Christ, we can never become the best we can truly be.

According to the world, our worth is defined by our achievements, relationship status, physical appearance or financial status. Ladies, know that all these things are fleeting so we must accept that our worth is found in who God says we are. I came across this quote over a year ago, and it totally shifted my perspective "We're a girl by birth, woman by maturity but lady by choice."

If we are going to truly believe we are royalty, we have to realize that the way we've been cultured by the world cannot be the same way we operate in the kingdom of God. That's why Colossians 3:2 says to put on the mind of Christ because we must choose to become ladies and not settle to be just "women." Get this, we are all women and that's not a bad thing. A lady is not "better" than a woman; she's simply "set apart." Romans 12:2 has called us to not conform to the pattern of this world but instead renew our minds and conform to God's standards.

So who's a lady? A lady is a woman of redefined behavior and speech. In our case, the Word of God, which now becomes our standard, redefines us. A woman is characterized by femininity but being a lady encompasses both our inward and outward disposition. Modesty, mannerism and courtesy are a part of a lady's trait. Ladies are adaptable, confident, purpose-driven, possess a positive outlook on life, and are lifelong learners. A lady is not weak, perfect or boastful. Because of the mind of Christ, we are empowered by the Holy Spirit. A lady knows that because we're made in God's image (Genesis 1:26), we can reflect Christ's character through our love, patience, forgiveness, and kindness.

Honestly, I didn't consider myself a true "lady" because I was a bit of a "tom-boy" plus, I thought being a lady meant I could not be myself (fun, relaxed, and imperfect). However, God has truly been renewing my mind, and I'm accepting myself, flaws and all. God called me into royalty and it's up to me to accept my new identity. My sister, no matter what age you are, you can start living a royal reality. The world needs more ladies! Here are three ways you can cultivate this in your life:

1. **Think Like Jesus.** We need to take control of our thoughts. The mind is very powerful and our reality is formed from the thoughts we have (Romans 8:6), whether we are defeated or victorious we must think positive and think godly. Philippians 4:8 says, "Finally, brethren, whatsoever things are true, whatsoever things are honest, whatsoever things are just, whatsoever things are pure, whatsoever things are lovely, whatsoever things are of good report; if there be any virtue, and if there be any praise, think on these things." You must guard your heart by being mindful of what you watch, read, and listen to. These things plant seeds (thoughts) in your mind and if you're not careful, they can become your ways.

2. **Embrace God's Love.** We often try to earn God's love by following laws to "prove" we love Him. God is love (1 John 4:8). You cannot earn it—you must embrace it. When we do this, then our actions won't be done to gain a reward simply out of obedience. Know that nothing you have done or can do will separate you from His love. James 4:8 says, "Draw close to God and he will draw close to you." So fall in love with God through praise, worship, prayer, reading His Word and spending time with Him. The more you embrace His love; you will realize that you start to hate things He hates and love what He loves. (Isaiah 54:10)

3. **Desire to be Holy.** Holiness means being fully devoted to God, set aside for His special use and set apart from sin and its influence. 1 Peter 1:16 says: "You must be holy because I am holy." We will always try to make the excuse that we are not perfect, which is true, but we must desire what God desires. Holiness will cause us to be separated from the world. We cannot achieve holiness on our own, God has given us the Holy Spirit to help us obey and give us the power to overcome sin. Holiness is not an external change, but it's internal (a heart matter), which will lead to outward manifestations. This lifelong

process happens as we grow in intimacy with Christ. The only way we can truly impact the world is by being separate, not by compromise.

"Renewing Your Mind" Tidbits:

- A change of mind leads to a change of experience.
- Understand the way the mind works and you will understand why things are the way they are.
- The way you think determines the way you act. The way you act determines your habit. And your habits determine your experiences.
- What you hear repeatedly, you will eventually believe.
- Guard your eyes. Guard your mind. Guard your heart. Guard your ears.

We are called to be like Christ—this is a lifelong journey and the process can be discouraging. We might be faced with persecution and distractions may slow us down, but we should never give up. Keep moving forward even if you feel you've missed the mark. We must be imitations of Him, which can only be achieved when we put off the old man and pursue the things of God. Don't be caught up with the worldly pursuits, instead, believe that you can always call upon God.

Chapter 14:

It's Not About Us

Royal Affirmation
"I will forget myself long enough to serve others."
(Philippians 2:4)

The Word of God says that we're God's royalty, heirs of God's kingdom and heirs with Christ. Therefore, we are called to live like His royalty and not just accept the title. Unfortunately, many people have a false perception of what it means to live like royalty. They live for themselves and put themselves on a pedestal above others, allowing pride and conceit to control them. This is not how Jesus wants us to live. Godly royalty isn't about living for ourselves or pretending we are better than others while competing with others for attention and rewards. Living a royal reality is about living in obedience to God's Word and spreading the truth of God's Word to all who are lost.

When I first became a Christian, I got caught up in pursuing worldly success and I wasn't concerned about eternity or fulfilling God's purpose for my life. I felt I needed a nice husband, car, house, beautiful children, a doctorate and a top management position making good money while still serving in some ministries. These things were my focus until one night when I was truly seeking God after experiencing some spiritual attacks. God said, "Crystal my people are lost, my people need help, my people need Jesus. The harvest is plentiful but the laborers are few. There aren't enough people willing to serve in my kingdom." Too many of us are focused on ourselves.

We live in such a broken world. Every day, babies are dying of hunger, there are car accidents, and people are being killed all over the world for choosing Jesus. Millions of babies are being aborted. Females are forced into drugs, sex trafficking and are raped. The HIV/AIDS rates are rising and more homosexual laws are taking over. Devotions and prayers are no longer allowed in schools... The world is coming to an end; yet, many people focus their attention on shows like Scandal, Keeping up With the Kardashian's, The Grammy's, and the Tabloids. You have to realize that the world needs you. The world needs servants.

The world needs your gifts, talents, prayers, money, time, and most importantly your obedience. Even as we come into the true knowledge of who God says we are, accept our identity, discover our purpose, and pursue our God–given dreams, we must keep in mind that life is not about us. It's not about you! It's not about me! Our obedience to truly be God's hands and feet on this earth is needed. We were not created to be selfish but we need each other. A true royalty has a servant's heart. In the world, success is measured by prestige but in God's kingdom success is measured by service. A heart for service is a true heart of royalty. It's never about personal gain but about glorifying God with all aspects of your life. Royalties make themselves available to be used by God. A servant is always willing to help others and do the best with what they have. As a royalty, we live for the audience of one and not for the approval of others. We can serve and give unselfishly without self-promotion or trying to impress others. We are created to serve (Ephesians 2:10).

So each of us has a part to play, we can't only be concerned about ourselves. Our lives must include devotion to others and we must seek to please, honor, and give our best to our Father's business.

We can serve wherever God leads because our identity is in Christ—not our position, prestige, qualification or power. As royalties, we know we serve God by serving others. We serve by sharing the gospel every chance we get, we serve by giving financially to people in need, we serve by giving time, gifts, and talents for kingdom building, we serve by praying for others, we serve by simply helping others. So whatever you have, know that God wants you to use it, not for yourself, but to benefit others.

Chapter 15:

It's a Faith Walk

Royal Affirmation

"I will walk by faith and not by sight."

(2 Corinthians 5:7)

In life, there are two realities: God's reality versus our reality. The question is which is more "real"? In our reality, we only believe what we can see, feel, hear, touch, and smell. If it doesn't satisfy our senses then we want to reject it. Unfortunately, reality for us can also be very daunting because when we look around at the various wars, the ill-effects of society, and our many negative experiences, it has an effect on how we view the sovereign limitless God.

On the contrary, God's reality, also considered the kingdom, is not physical. It is powerful (1 Corinthians 4:20), unshakable (Hebrews 12:28), and invisible. In living a royal reality, we have to understand how both realities co-exist. If we operate in our reality, then we are operating by the flesh and we know that leads to death. This is not just a physical death but the death of our purpose, dreams, identity and destiny. If we operate in God's "reality" then we are choosing to walk by faith and operate under the spirit, which gives life, peace, and joy.

Royalties, know this is a faith walk—faith spans over both realities because God has given each of us a seed of faith but it's up to us to cultivate it. So the more you exercise your faith, the more it grows. Faith is reality before we see it. Faith overcomes doubt, fear, and anxiety (1 John 5:4), it is a gift from God (Romans 12:3), it pleases God (Hebrews 11:6), and it releases us into all the provisions of God (Galatians 3:9).

Many people underestimate the power of faith; but we should realize that faith is not about how, it's about who! The "who" is the eternal, immutable, infinite, omnipotent creator of the universe. He is faithful and that means everything that Jehovah Abba has promised us will come to pass. Faith comes by hearing the Word of God, so if He says it then it is so. If our knowledge of God is limited and our relationship is weak, then our faith will also be limited and weak. Faith is a consistent and unwavering confidence in God. For God to operate in our lives, we must believe. Believe that ALL things are possible with God (Matthew 19: 28); if God can then I can (Philippians 4:13); if God is calling me to do it, then it's already done because He has already enabled me to do it (1 John 5:4-5).

One of my favorite definitions of faith is "Calling beyond the visible into the invisible and taking hold of what God says is yours, and not letting go until you pull it down from out of the invisible into the visible"- Pastor Peter Malcolm. God's reality is invisible, but it is more real than what we can see because everything came about through the spoken word of God. In other words, in God's reality, we must believe before we can see.

Royalties, I want us to understand that in order for us to truly live a faithful life, become the best God has called us to be, operate in our purpose, achieve our dreams and prepare for eternity; is through faith. The fact is, when people say they don't believe in God, it's because they refuse to accept that what we see in the natural is temporary and only the things that we cannot see will last for eternity. This is why many people want to disprove the Trinity because it doesn't make sense in the human mind; they say hell doesn't exist because the god they created in their head is good but not just. They want to work and do good things to earn their salvation when God says its simple faith in Jesus Christ that gives us this gift. Many want to use parts of the Bible (The Word of God) to satisfy their own desires and theories but refuse the part that doesn't fit their lifestyle or their pride won't allow them to accept.

One of my top spiritual gifts is faith and God has used my testimonies to inspire others to believe in His promises, power, and presence. I can give many accounts of God's faithfulness in my life but for now I will share two short testimonies with you. I truly pray that it encourages someone to start believing that God is truly faithful.

First of all, I came from a low-income family and to get a degree seemed like a dream. No one in my family had ever attended a university, but I was determined to get my degree. I applied, got accepted, and of course—I had no funds. I prayed and I trusted that God would not fail me and He didn't. In 2008, I met someone (I'll say an angel) who decided that he wanted to help fund my college education with no strings attached. He financed the majority of my college degree and for the rest of the tuition he didn't pay for, I got an unexpected scholarship to cover. You might think I am exaggerating, but I did not know the person. I met him via social media, spoke to him a few times and just like that, God used him to bless me. We are now very good friends and he's a trusted mentor to me. I knew, and my family knew that we would not have been able to afford to get a college degree, but God is truly faithful.

Then, at age 24, I bought an apartment. My salary was not enough to pay a mortgage, my bank account definitely did not have the funds for even a deposit on an apartment, and I certainly didn't win the lotto. A close friend of mine urged me to apply for the apartment but I didn't. However, she completed the form and dropped it off. I was shocked to be called for an interview. Honestly, it seemed impossible. I was 24 years old, a single mother, and worked a simple accounting job but the favor of God was truly on me. My church family prayed, I prayed, and honestly, I cried so much when I finally got my keys.

I only paid $35 US dollars for the deposit and had no fees at all. After I got the apartment and the mortgage payment came out of my salary, I had $20 US dollars to survive on monthly. For 7 months until I got a new job, God supernaturally provided. He paid all of my bills and provided groceries, clothes, and furniture. I truly learned that my job was not my source, but God is truly a provider, sustainer, deliverer--my all in all.

I could share many other testimonies of acquiring jobs that I seemingly wasn't qualified for. Going on overseas trips that I didn't buy plane tickets for, getting a car, and even getting this book published were all a part of my walk of faith. God had these blessings set aside for me in the spiritual realm and my faith pulled them down in the physical realm. God is so real! God is Faithful!

My sister, I'm sure that I'm no more special than you are to God. He loves us all equally (Galatians 3:28). So whatever He has in store for you, you can receive it, but it is through your faith that your blessings will come.

Honestly, I have no steps to give you about walking in faith because it's something that comes naturally. Faith comes by hearing the Word, so the more you meditate on scriptures, listen to Christian motivational videos and read godly books, the deeper your faith will become. We all have been given a measure of faith, so we should build on this by applying faith in little things so that our faith will begin to work in greater things. I won't say everything I've had faith for came into fruition because that's not true. One of my biggest disappointments was starting my MBA in faith but not being able to complete it due to a lack of financial resources. The beautiful thing about faith in God is that even when I'm disappointed, it doesn't change who He is and my faith is not hindered by my feelings, my faith is in GOD Himself. So I trust that His plans are greater and possible. If it's His will, I will complete my MBA and even Doctorate.

So my advice royalties, is to just start walking by faith. It means you cannot depend on yourself (Proverbs 3:5), it means surrendering to God, putting God first in your life, believing in His Word (promises), listening to the Holy Spirit and resting in His love.

Chapter 16:

Choose to Live Your God-Given Dream

Royal Affirmation

"I know my God can do exceedingly abundantly more than I can imagine." (Ephesians 3:20)

I've always been a dreamer. In my younger years, I would change my career goals every year based on my subjects or new interests. One thing I've noticed though is that no matter what I thought I wanted to be—helping people has always been my deepest desire.

My social background appeared to have placed limitations on many of my dreams, so things like getting a Bachelor's degree, being in top management, speaking at different events to motivate people or helping my family come out of the inner-city wouldn't seem possible based on my physical and financial constraints. But no matter how things appeared—I never stopped dreaming!

I've met many young ladies and have many friends who aborted their dreams because they thought it wasn't possible to achieve them. Some days, I got discouraged and thought maybe I could not achieve some things but honestly, one verse that I would always recite is: "I can do ALL things through Christ who gives me strength" (Philippians 4:13).

God places dreams in our hearts to show His faithfulness. I won't say every dream or desire is God-given because many peoples' dreams are driven by pride, jealousy, envy, greed or other selfish motives; I don't believe God will "bless" mess.

I do believe that we have dreams with pure motives. With determination, faith, and zero-tolerance to excuses, we can achieve our goals and God can exceed our expectations. Goals are simply dreams with deadlines.

In my personal life, God has shown His faithfulness and omnipotent power over and over. God has literally blown me away! I cannot take credit for anything I have achieved. I have truly done nothing. I dream, do all I can do (plan, research possibilities and pray without ceasing), step out in faith and watch God do what only He can do.

Don't get me wrong, I haven't received everything I asked God for but that's the beautiful thing about having a relationship with the King. I trust that His plans for me are good, and He will not withhold any good thing from me; so if He doesn't give me something—I know it is either not the right time or it's not His best.

"We are each responsible for our own conduct." – *Galatians 6:5*

Many times, our dreams don't come to pass, and it's not necessarily because we aren't smart enough or spiritual enough; it's simply because we're unwilling to take the necessary risks to achieve them. We lack faith and without faith—it's impossible to please God. Faith turns dreams into reality. Nothing happens until we start dreaming.

Some people are stuck playing the blame game. They blame everything on their circumstances and their failures, but our choices have just as much impact. We cannot control our circumstances, but we can control how we respond. Choosers do what it takes to live their dreams. Your choices have a greater impact on your ability to achieve your dreams than any other competing factor.

Too many people put their dreams on hold because:

1. They settle for what life has handed to them and get complacent with where they are.

2. They get stuck in a job that they don't like and discouragement takes over so they no longer feel motivated.

3. They allow excuses, doubts and fear to conquer them.

4. They listen to dream killers and naysayers who feed them lies.

5. They allow their feelings of insecurity rob them of opportunities.

6. They allow circumstances and conditions to convince them that they don't deserve a better life.

7. They sit waiting on perfect conditions, which leads to procrastination.

Today, I want to tell you to shake off those feelings! Don't accept those lies for one more day. No matter what situations you find yourself in, take charge of your destiny and start living out your dreams today.

In Living a Royal Reality, you must make the choice to pursue your God-given dreams. Big dreams show that you have faith in a BIG GOD! It shows your trust and reliance on Him.

We must surrender our dreams to God. Matthew 16:25 states: *"If you give up your life for Christ's sake, you will find it."* So first ask God to take away any dream that is not of Him and replace it with His dreams that align with His purpose and calling for your life. *Ephesians 3:20* says: "God can do exceedingly, abundantly more than we can imagine in our wildest dreams." Therefore, trust that God's dream for your life is significantly bigger than yours and is of eternal value. So, I ask you, if you could have one dream come through in your life, what would it be?

Three ways to know if a dream is from God are:

1. It will be connected to your purpose, which ultimately glorifies Him. This means our motives must be checked. We must ensure our dream is not to compete with anyone else or birthed out of a heart of covetousness. A God-given dream will help shape you into a better person.

2. It seems impossible to come to pass on your own strength. This will require an act of faith, and we know without faith, it is impossible to please God. Therefore, the bigger our faith, the more pleased God is with us.

3. It's a desire that grows bigger overtime. Many times we're pressed to do something, but we delay and make excuses for why we shouldn't. Remember, delayed obedience is disobedience. God has given us tasks to do, and we should not hesitate. Someone is depending on your obedience.

Royalties, never let a seemingly impossible situation intimidate you. Let it motivate you to seek God more, pray more, believe more, and trust more. Start dreaming great dreams for God.

Chapter 17:

Living for Eternity

Royal Affirmation

"I know this world is not my home, and I'm looking forward to my everlasting home in heaven."
(Hebrews 13:14)

In Living A Royal Reality, you live for a greater purpose than what is around you. How you live now will determine where you spend your eternity. Our relationship with God determines if we will be united with Him in heaven or separated from Him and cast away to hell.

As royalties, we must accept that this life on earth is temporary. When our hearts stop beating, our bodies and time on earth will expire but the soul and spirit live on. God has entrusted us with certain "things" to manage on this earth, and He will hold us accountable for them. We must understand we are simply stewards of all the things God has given us because God owns ALL things. Psalms 24:1 says: "The earth is the Lord's and all its fullness, the world and those who are here." God has blessed us with these things so we can use them for His purpose and for His glory.

If we think about eternity more than we think about the earth, the decisions we make daily as we face our realities will be different. As royalties, we know that our true home is not of this world. So, we think differently from unbelievers who are busy storing up treasures here on this earth. We know our Father lives in heaven and that's where our permanent home is (James 4:4 & 1 Peter 1:17).

When we start living for eternity, we will realize that when certain tragedies hit, unanswered prayers and disappointments occur, we're able to cope because we will never be totally fulfilled on this earth anyway. We understand that we were created for far more and that eternity awaits us.

Jesus told us that he has gone to prepare a place for us (John 14:3). If this life on earth is all we care about, we are in trouble because all the riches, fame, and things of this world are temporary. Many people think that the God of love will not send anyone to hell and some people even think they are experiencing hell already. Some believe that as long as you are a "good" person you will go to heaven but the scriptures prove that all of those beliefs are flawed.

We know we are all sinners and the wages of sin is death (eternal separation from God) (Romans 6:23). God became man, took the punishment for us and "paid the price" for our sins (John 3:16). So only those who place their faith in the Lord Jesus Christ (Acts 16:3 & Romans 10:9); repent from their old lives and set their course to follow Christ (Mark 8:34); serve God with a grateful heart (Psalm 100:2); and allow God to transform their lives (1 John 3:9-10) shall be allowed in heaven. God is holy and perfect, and He cannot allow unrighteousness to enter His dwelling place. Only the blood of Jesus can wash and sanctify us to be acceptable to enter heaven.

Royalty, do not be deceived into believing that the earth is your home and all the things you have earned are yours. Don't be deceived into thinking that heaven or hell does not exist. It would be sad for you to hear the Gospel of Jesus Christ over and over and continue rejecting it, then on judgment day hear: "Depart from me, I never knew you" (Matthew 7:23). We cannot get too attached to what's around us because all of it is temporary. Nothing is wrong with achieving nice things or being successful, but we must check our motives because the most important thing in life is to have a relationship with God. Of course, it won't be easy because sin is so tempting but keeping your focus on eternity will help.

We must live godly and holy lives while we are waiting on God. This is a major part of living a royal reality. That means when life gets rough, and we're overwhelmed by the troubles of this world, we should remember our home is not here—there is far greater on the other side of death.

Chapter 18:

For Such a Time as This

Royal Affirmation
"I am CALLED for Such A Time As This."
(Esther 4:14)

I must confess, writing this book was truly a test of faith. To reveal so much of my life to possibly millions of people was really challenging but I had to continue reminding myself, I live to please an audience of "ONE" and that's my Abba Daddy. Living a Royal Reality continues… I'm still learning so much about kingdom life and I know I will continue to be made perfect in His eyes as I press towards the mark.

I've tried for many years to fit in, but I'm finally accepting that I was made to stand out and I'm royalty, so are you.

God has called you (2 Timothy 1:9), redeemed you (Ephesians 1:7) and chosen you (Ephesians 1:4) for such a time as this…

As royalties, God has asked us to leave empty pursuits, shallow distractions and build our lives around His priorities. This doesn't just mean having our own relationship with Christ; it also means becoming His light in this dying world. We cannot just build our lives around our own pursuits and comforts, but we are commissioned to share the Gospel and serve wherever He leads us.

The saying, "For Such A Time as this" means our time has come to truly impact the world for the glory of God. We already possess the power to overcome our challenges so let's move on from our past and start preparing for eternity. Regardless of how our "realities" look, we can change our worldview by walking by faith in God's reality.

If you haven't accepted Jesus Christ as your personal Lord and Savior, then you aren't living a Royal Reality…

If you would like to have a relationship with God, the first step is to acknowledge that we have all sinned and that there is nothing we can do to earn God's love (Romans 3:23-28). Then we must believe and confess that Jesus is Lord (Romans 10:9) and allow Him to guide our lives.

The proud human heart finds it difficult to accept that salvation is so simple. Most of us keep trying to be better in our own human strength. We must accept that we cannot gain victory over sin and walk into our brand new life of freedom on our own—only God can do it for us. It takes a moment to become a Christian but to remain a Christian is a life-long process of becoming who God has called you to be (discovering your purpose). Salvation is more than a happy feeling. It is the willingness to submit to Christ as He lives out His life within us.

"But because of His great love for us, God, who is rich in mercy, made us alive with Christ even when we were dead in transgressions - it is by grace you have been saved." - Ephesians 2:4-5

If you would like to accept Jesus as Lord of your life, you can pray the following prayer:

"Lord, I confess that I have sinned against You and ask You to forgive me. I am sorry that my sins have hurt You and other people in my life. I acknowledge that I could never earn salvation by my good works, but I come to You and trust in what Jesus did for me on the cross. I believe that You love me and that Jesus died and rose again so that I can be forgiven and come to know You. I ask You to come into my heart and be Lord of my life. I trust You with everything, and I thank You for loving me so much that I can know You here on earth and spend the rest of eternity with You in heaven. In Jesus name, Amen."

This is the beginning of your new birth, the beginning of your new life in the royal family. To help you grow in Christ:

1. Tell someone (pastor or Christian friend) who can help you find your gift to serve.
2. Get baptized.
3. Join a Bible preaching church.
4. Pray and read your Bible daily.
5. Seek a godly mentor.
6. Listen to godly preachers in your spare time.
7. Be mindful of what you feed yourself.
8. Join a women's ministry, pinky promise group or I'm Royal movement for sisterhood and support.

If you are already a believer, continue to grow in the Lord. Are you truly becoming who you are so you can become ALL that you can be? Ask yourself, does everything I do reflect my Royal identity? It is not enough to say you are royal, but we should speak, look and most of all reflect who our King is. Know that where you are positioned now, is for a purpose. There is something to learn and something to contribute.

Life is a journey. There will be days of chaos and other times, you will wear your confidence with a smile. Sometimes life might not seem fair because things are thrown at you that you might not believe you deserve. Remember, GOD is in charge and once He allows it, He has already prepared us to handle it. You might not believe it based on how we feel at the time, but feelings are temporary. However, God's plans are eternal. Trust that God is with you, that He will never leave you nor forsake you, and that He will work it all together for your good.

Start seeing yourself as God sees you. We have to see ourselves as forgiven. We have to see ourselves as healed. We have to see ourselves as delivered. Until we can see ourselves the way God sees us, we can never truly walk in the fullness of His love and the gift of life that He has given us.

Woman of God, walk with confidence and stand strong. A virtuous woman lives inside of you, use your potential and don't ever let anyone tell you that you're not good enough. Remember under God's protective royalty, the Devil, your enemy cannot touch you. You're a daughter of the King, a beautiful princess with an unfailing crown.

Royalties, the journey continues…
God loves you and I love you too.

www.ingramcontent.com/pod-product-compliance
Lightning Source LLC
Chambersburg PA
CBHW070454100426
42743CB00010B/1617